COLOURING the RAINBOW

Mauritian Society in the Making

edited by
Marina Carter

CRIOS
CENTRE FOR RESEARCH ON
INDIAN OCEAN SOCIETIES

Cover Illustration:
Painting by Leroy (1860)

Layout and Cover Design:
Khalil Muthy

Photographs:
Mahendra Koreemun

Published by
Centre for Research on Indian Ocean Societies
PO Box 138, Port Louis

Printed by
Alfran Co Ltd, Mauritius

ISBN: 99903-52-00-3

Contents

Preface

This book is the first publication to appear under the auspices of the Centre for Research on Indian Ocean Societies (CRIOS), an organisation created in 1997 by a group of Mauritian and foreign social scientists with a common interest in the region.

It is also the second in the 'Rainbow' series, now an ongoing project of CRIOS. The first volume in the series, *Forging the Rainbow: Labour Immigrants in British Mauritius*, dealt with the streams of labour immigration which brought Indian, Chinese, Malagasy, Comorian and Mozambican workers to the island during the 19th century. The present volume highlights the inter-relationships which have served to facilitate the implantation of the successive waves of immigrants into French and British Mauritius. Further volumes are currently in preparation.

I would like to thank the following:

- The Ministry of Arts & Culture for financial sponsorship of this publication
- The staff of the Mauritius Archives and the Mahatma Gandhi Institute
- My fellow contributors and particularly James Ng Foong Kwong for his help in the conceptualisation and realisation of this book
- Mr Patrick Eisenlohn and Ms Tania Dræbel for their critical reading of earlier drafts
- Dr Sheila Bunwaree-Ramharai, Ms Nita Deerpalsing and Mrs Saloni Deerpalsingh for their encouragement and support
- Mr Khalil Muthy for the design and layout, and Alfran Co Ltée for printing, of the book
- My friends and family in Mauritius and England.

Marina Carter
January 1998

Introduction

Any nation is a field of contesting ideologies, but in Mauritius this is particularly apparent because of the lack of a clear single-identity hegemony. There is a marked discrepancy between the co-operation among Mauritians and the competition between ethnic groups which still prevails. This latent tension has been nourished by the persistence of ethnic myths enmeshed in the written and popular history of Mauritius which helps to perpetuate such modern social division. Yet the lived history of Mauritians has been and still is one of adaptation and co-existence. The present study represents a modest attempt to address some of the lacunae in modern Mauritian studies and, to illustrate the development of such inter-relations, introduces the concept of 'creoledom'. *Creoledom* is defined as the processes of conflict, co-operation and adaptation in which settlers engaged whilst integrating into an island society. Creoledom is explored in the present volume through discussions of the integration of Indian convicts and labour immigrants, the formation of new social groups through inter-marriage, such as the free Coloureds, the Creole-Chinese, and the Afro-Creoles, and the elaboration of 'communities' through the absorption of minorities into larger social entities.

Mauritian history, as it has been written until quite recently, has been overweighted in favour of official documents, press accounts, and the lives of important figures - the world of the ordinary person has been forgotten. Classics of Mauritian history, such as the work of Auguste Toussaint, have continued to be used as tools of reference; few attempts have been made to incorporate the mass of information which can be gleaned from non-official sources. Yet such documentation can not only shed new light but can lead to fundamental reinterpretations of the several phases of settlement of the island. Thus Toussaint's compilation of official sources remains an indispensable research tool, but as a point of departure for an understanding of Asian immigration, its usefulness is limited. Those works which deal with single ethnic groups have additionally tended to be written from a community-oriented viewpoint: Emrith's work on Muslims (1994) and Sooriamoorthy's volume about Tamils (1977) fall into this category. Doctoral-based single-community studies, such as *La Diaspora Chinoise dans l'océan Indien Occidental* of Ly Tio Fane (1983), are more useful as historical models.

Recent historical research which has made use of new sources to challenge the colonial discourse has revitalised Mauritian studies. Allen (1983) has demonstrated that notarial records can reveal trends of co-operation in capital accumulation which is scarcely documented in official correspondence, Jumeer (1984) has used police records to document the organisation of 'libre' society in the 18th century, and Teelock (1995) has begun to recreate slave genealogies. Slaves, free coloureds and indentured Indians made depositions before police magistrates, courts of justice and committees of enquiry which, despite the inaccuracies of their transcription, and the often vested interests they were made to serve, have proved to be a vital source for the historian (Jumeer, 1984; Teelock, 1995; Carter, 1996). More literate or more well-off immigrants had recourse to petitions which enabled them to express their grievances in an unconstrained manner to the colonial authorities, and even to reach the ear of the Governor. Two works have sought to provide new insights into the lives of Indian women and Chinese traders respectively, using petitions as a major source (Carter, 1994; Ng, 1996). Whilst individual studies are beginning to redress some of the gaps in Mauritian historiography, particularly the recapturing of the voiceless in history, others are challenging the replication in historical discourse of the xenophobia of 19th century newspaper journalists, the racial prejudices of colonial administrators, the cultural ignorance of contemporary commentators, and the filio-pietism of single-community studies. Ng (1996) has described in detail the construction of anti-Chinese sentiments in 19th century Mauritius as articulated in the press and Callikhan-Proag (1984) has similarly evoked changing attitudes towards Indian immigrants in her work.

The purpose of this volume is to explore these themes further. The first article discusses the origins of cultural diversity in the settlement of the Isle of France, and assesses the gap between policy and practice in the burgeoning relationships between ethnic groups which were divided juridically and socially. The paper also exposes the hollowness of ethnic stereotypes which were then current and which have been reproduced in later historical works. D'Unienville's article continues the theme of unravelling the complex relationships between White colonists and Black slaves, and between planters of different ethnic groups. The historical vignettes presented reveal the surprising acts of heroism and support which are part and parcel of the human experience but which sit uneasily within general accounts of group antagonisms.

D'Unienville's article draws attention to the spirit of mutual dependence which has always characterised the various components of colonial society despite the divisions of power and authority which seperate them. Capital is notoriously disrespectful of ethnic and class barriers - and it was Muslim merchants among others, who, helped to finance the Hindu land acquisitions of the *petit* and *grand morcellements*. The Chinese, unable to purchase land because of their status as aliens, found a solution to this problem by leasing property from the Indian landowners who emerged as a result of the 19th century morcellements. These two groups also co-operated in the development of commerce in the capital. Chinese shopkeepers provided a link between diverse communities in Mauritius. Ahine, who owned more than six boutiques in the mid 1840s, served customers as diverse as indentured Indian labourers, Creoles, and White Mauritians in different localities of the capital. Thus, Chinese and Indians in the commercial sector worked with Creole and White traders, to their mutual benefit. Those White and Creole importers and wholesalers of merchandise who saw in the Chinese retailers, not adversaries, but collaborators in the distribution and sale of their goods across the country, were able to benefit from the spread of commercial activities which Chinese traders brought to Mauritius. In this way, the development of economic inter-dependence between various groups in Mauritian society was prefigured (Carter & Ng in this volume).

Anderson's paper reveals how a small community - the Indian convicts - evaded proscriptions restricting their contacts with the wider society to engage in economic activities and social relationships with other groups. In this way, the convicts successfully integrated with both the Creole and Indian communities in 19th century Mauritius. African immigrants were also co-opted into Creole society through intermarriage, leading to the gradual disappearance of distinctive traits, in much the same way that Bengali speakers, tribals and other minorities within the Indian community also effectively disappear from sight over the same period (Carter, and

Carter & Govinden in this volume). The labour immigrations which transformed the demographic structure of 19th century Mauritius cannot be read purely in terms of employer tactics of divide and rule using ethnic differences as a weapon (although this strategy was certainly in play); labour history in Mauritius has its stories of co-operation across ethnic lines.

This inter-ethnic co-operation is exemplified by Ng's article which shows the crucial role played by Creoles in the establishment of the first Chinese traders in Mauritius. He stresses the support provided by Creole women partners of Chinese men and demonstrates that the offspring of these alliances - and the forerunners of the Creole-Chinese community - carved an important niche for themselves in society. In this way a new social category was formed out of the fortuitous inter-relationships of Creole women and Chinese men.

Communities, which have tended to be perceived as homogenous entities in Mauritian historiography, are, on closer inspection, revealed to be fraught with internal divisions. Carter & Govinden demonstrate that the Indian community was itself constantly being redefined in Mauritius through inter-marriage and through the absorption of small ethnic and linguistic groups into the larger sub-groupings. The Chinese in Mauritius also differentiated themselves between those who entered as contract labour, and those who arrived as free immigrants with the intention to become traders (Carter & Ng, 1997). Recent research on the Muslims in Mauritius tells a similar story of internal class and ethnic based differences (Jahangeer-Chojoo, 1997). Increasingly Mauritian researchers are prepared to debate such characteristics and in so doing to unravel some of the complexities of local ethnology. Even those pillars of community-identification, the annual religious festivals of Mauritians, have always been, and continue to be, amended to the particular characteristics of Mauritian society and participated in by several ethnic groups (Ramhota & Govinden in this volume). It is towards such understandings of the foundation of Mauritian society, and in particular, the economic and cultural interactions which are at the heart of *creoledom*, that the contributors to this book draw attention.

Founding an Island Society: Inter-Ethnic Relationships in the Isle of France

Marina Carter

Bernardin de St Pierre, wrote, in the 18th century, of the pleasure of witnessing the human diversity of the Isle of France:

> *quel plaisir... de voir là le noir de Guinée cultiver ses bananiers, là le noir de Madagascar cueillir le grain de ses coffiers, dans un autre verger la fille du Bengale cueillir ses cannes de sucre, une bergère caffre conduire ses troupeaux dans les forêts et chanter. Ici la Malabare file ses cotons à l'ombre des bananiers, là la Bengale fait des toiles et les vallons retentissent des chants de ces diverses nations répétés par les échos. Ah! si les concerts des voix des oiseaux différents sont si charmants dans les forêts, combien les voix des hommes de diverses nations dans le même paysage.* (p. 436).

This diversity was predicated on the nature of the settlement of the new colony: its peopling was sporadic and the ships which each unloaded a few individuals from the disparate ports they had called at, produced an early society composed of Guinées, Malays, Tamils and Bengalis, as well as French settlers. It was not until the late 18th century that organised slaving voyages created a predominance of Malagasy and Mozambican labourers. To reinforce hierarchical divisions of status and colour, legislation was promulgated to restrict contact between groups. Relationships which crossed these divides thus became illicit, but informal unions were widespread, and formalised when circumstances permitted, such as during the Revolutionary years.

Social Apartheid and its Evaders

The Isle of France was, in the 18th century, a slave colony regulated by the Code Noir, controlled initially by the French East India Company and later by the Royal Government. It was a hierarchical society composed of three classes - Whites, free Coloureds and slaves, groups which were further differentiated by ethnic origin and religious belief. The colonial state entrenched divisions between free and slave through legislation which restricted intermarriage and the harbouring of deserters.

The Code Noir, applied to the Isles of France and Bourbon through the Lettres Patentes of September 1724, clearly prohibited marriage and even unofficial sexual relationships between the different groups of 'blancs', 'libres' and 'esclaves' (Whites, free Coloureds and slaves). Article V ordained:

> *Défendons à nos sujets blancs de l'un et de l'autre sexe de contracter mariage avec les Noirs, à peine de punition et d'amende arbitraire, ... défendons aussi à nos dits sujets blancs, même aux Noirs affranchis ou nés libres, de vivre en concubinage avec des esclaves; voulons que ceux qui auront eu un ou plusieurs enfans d'une pareille conjonction, ensemble les maîtres qui les auront soufferts, soient condamnés chacun en une amende de trois cents livres et s'ils sont maîtres de l'esclave de laquelle ils auront eu lesdits enfans, voulons qu'outre l'amende ils soient privés tant de l'esclave que des enfans, et qu'ils soient adjugés à l'hôpital des lieux, sans pouvoir jamais être affranchis; n'entendons toutefois le présent article avoir lieu lorsque l'homme noir affranchi ou libre qui n'était pas marié durant son concubinage avec son esclave, épousera dans les formes prescrites par l'église, ladite esclave, qui sera affranchie par ce moyen, et les enfans rendus libres et légitimes.* (Noel, 1991: 163-177)

Commenting on the provisions of the Lettres Patentes, Raymond d'Unienville writes 'C'était déjà, tout au moins sur papier, un genre d'apartheid'. He further notes that the harsh provisions of this law were reaffirmed in 1771 when the Ministre de la Marine wrote 'qu'en aucun cas, à aucun degré de métissage, un descendant de nègre ne pouvait escompter devenir un 'citoyen' du royaume' (d'Unienville, 1979b: 37).

Alongside state imposed limitations on inter-ethnic contact, a range of stereotypes was current, which differentiated ethnic groups further, demarcating them to specific tasks or roles, according to perceived aptitudes and characteristics. The Malagasys in the Isle of France were described as prone to marronnage, and as being inordinately fond of women; Mozambicans were considered to be good, obedient field workers and Indians were depicted as docile, garrulous, neat in manners and appearance and ideally suited for domestic service (d'Unienville, 1885; Milbert, 1812).

Despite social stereotypes and juridical proscriptions, shared lifestyles and common ethnicity frequently broke down the barriers which separated the different groups. It is clear that in the Isle of France relations between Whites, free Coloureds and slaves were relatively fluid, and that the status gap between owners and slaves was further weakened by the shared ethnicity of many, and the cases of concubinage leading to enfranchisement and even marriage which occurred, usually between male owners and female slaves. The concessions allowed to the free coloured community included the right of non-Christians (principally Hindus) to own slaves. The Revolutionary period, which liberalised enfranchisement laws, also increased the numerical strength and political voice of the free coloured population, and even produced some documented marriages between Whites and their Coloured or freed concubines.

How was ethnic and social status conferred on individuals in the Isle of France? The validity of marriage data is complicated in the case of slaves by the fact that the Lettres Patentes prescribed that slaves could not marry without the consent of their masters and that children of slave marriages would also be slaves, and that they should belong to the owner of the mother rather than of the father. If a male slave married a free woman their children would be free like the mother, but if the father was free and the mother a slave, the children would also be considered slaves (articles vi-x). However married couples and their children could not be sold separately, if they belonged to the same owner (art xlii). Since the offspring took the status of the mother, be it free or slave, it seems likely that ethnicity of children was also passed on from the mother. The number of 'enfants naturels' exceeded that of 'enfants légitimes' both because civil marriage was not widespread, and because of the many cases where paternity could not be divulged, so it was the mother alone who was named as a parent. In practice, the baptismal and marriage records reveal the complexity of ethnic issues, and the multiplicity of 'caste' and 'nation' terms in use to describe and differentiate slaves and free persons of colour.

The discretion of civil status officers, and their brevity in recording parentage, is indicative of the 'gêne' surrounding relationships between different groups in the strictly hierarchically stratified society of the Isle of France. Yet contemporaries testify to the ubiquity of mixed relationships. Bernardin de Saint Pierre noted: 'Il y a très peu de gens mariés à la ville... la facilité de trouver des concubines parmi les Négresses en est la véritable raison' (p. 113). In 1764 a local priest, M. Teste, complained: 'C'est un bien grand désordre en l'Isle de France de voir des gens d'un certain rang entretenir publiquement des négresses, les équiper, leur fournir des logements et vivre de pair avec elles, les traiter comme des épouses, en avoir des enfants ... Ce mélange honteux a été introduit par le séjour des troupes de terre et de mer'. (Nagapen, 1996: 31).

Historians have to date had surprisingly little to say about this widespread social reality. Early historians such as Henri Prentout, described the relationships between slaves and slave-owners as having produced 'une caste mixte dite de sang-mêlé', and, writing in 1892, Evenor Hitié speculated about the sentiments which the fathers of such children might have felt for their offspring:

> *L'un mettait tous les enfants à la pioche sans pitié et les faisait fouetter sur une échelle, mode d'alors quand les esclaves manquaient au plus léger des devoirs qu'ils avaient à remplir. L'autre choisissait celui qui tenait de lui par la couleur et répandait quelque bonheur sur son enfance. Il fallait que cet enfant, devenu grand, se conduisit à la manière la plus exemplaire car à la plus petite faute, il était replongé dans la servitude, lui qui n'avait jamais cessé d'être esclave ... Un autre paraissait aimer ses enfants, quels qu'ils fussent, basanés ou blancs, semblait avoir de véritables entrailles de père pour eux, tout en les laissant croupir dans l'ignorance, mais, chose curieuse, détestait cordialement les enfants de couleur de ses meilleurs amis et répudiait la classe parmi laquelle se trouvaient ses fils ou ses filles comme viles misérables et dignes du plus profond mépris.* (quoted in Moutou, 1996: 136-7).

Toussaint, however, has commented that those Whites who 'se casèrent' with slaves, frequently enfranchised them in their wills, so that the women 'passaient du statut d'esclaves à celui de maîtresses' (Toussaint, 1979: 260). Taking the question one stage further, Nagapen has remarked on the different attitudes which prevailed among Whites in the Isle of France on this question: 'Si lcs négociants épousaient généralement des Franciliennes blanches, les marchands, quant à eux, choisissaient très souvent leurs compagnes parmi les libres de couleur'. These free persons of colour, enfranchised slaves or free immigrants, he adds, were juridically 'les égaux des blancs. Dans la réalité, ils ne l'étaient aucunement' (Nagapen, 1996: 36).

The extent of such relationships, and the efforts made by the partners in such relationships to do the best for themselves and their offspring in a system hostile to their very existence, have evidently remained comparatively unexplored to date, and an object of speculation rather than informed research. Yet, civil status, notarial and other documents provide a wealth of information about the mixed families of the Isle of France which can serve to illuminate the nature of colonial society itself.

Relationships between Whites, Coloureds and Slaves Before 1789

The pre-Revolutionary civil status records of the Isle of France are usually discreet on the subject of mixed relationships, the children of which were generally ascribed solely to the mother. It is possible, however, to chart such relationships through the designation of the offspring as *mulâtre*. Thus at Grand Port the birth of 'Joseph, mulâtre, fils naturel de Brigitte, indienne, esclave de Bonamour' was recorded. In some cases the mulâtrc offspring's paternity is alluded to. In July 1832 the baptism of the 8 day old Julien was recorded: 'un petit mulâtre fils d'Anne esclave indienne de Duplessis et d'un blanc inconnu'. Exceptionally, some fathers did recognise their offspring with slaves: in 1771 Marguerite Perrine, a four year old girl was baptised, and recorded as the 'fille naturelle of Nicolas Levaissère, Bourgeois, qui a reconnu cet enfant, et d'une négresse malgache libre'. In other cases the designation of the father as 'habitant' suffices to demonstrate the difference in civil status between the parents, as in June 1774 when the marriage in Port Louis was recorded of 'Michel Aloye fils mineur de Mathieu Aloye habitant, et Hélène Bastien négresse libre'. Family ties, although unstated, can be inferred from the presence of such 'habitants' at the ceremonies of their coloured relatives. Thus, when Jacques was baptised in 1781, he was stated to be the son of Marie Ursule Moutou and of 'Joseph dit Riou créol mulâtre libre'. The godfather of the child was Alexandre Riou, habitant à Poudre d'Or'.[1]

Notarial and enfranchisement records also rarely stated ties of paternity and concubinage between Whites and non-Whites, but in cases where individuals expressed a wish to leave all their property to their 'slave family', one can estimate the likelihood of blood-ties connecting them. When Yvon, *supercargue* of *Le Prince d'Orange*, went to Batavia in 1782, he left instructions that in case of his death, his female slave Marianne and her child should be liberated, and bequeathed 'une case de bazard' and a female slave. In addition 20,000 *livres* were to be allocated to the purchase of goods, the income from which was to be placed at her disposal. Yvon's executor was also directed to 'lui acheter une maison dans le Camp des noirs libres, à elle d'y loger, ou de la louer à sa volonté'. When the children were adult, this property was to become theirs on condition that their mother be accorded a pension. The rest of his property was bequeathed to his mother and sister. [2] Similarly the request of Jean Pitois to leave his property to the children of his slave Brigitte is couched in terms which typically suggest the closeness of their relationship:

> *Le nommé Jean Pitois dit St Prosper habitant au quartier de Flack accorde la liberté aux nommés Vincent âgé de neuf ans, François âgé de quatre ans, Françoise âgée de sept ans, à Marie Jeanne âgée de six ans, tous quatre enfans de défunte Brigitte négresse Madécasse son esclave, en considération des services distingués qu'elle lui avait rendus en son vivant, lui ayant sauvé la vie en trois occasions différentes ... ... en cas de décès du dit Pitois, sans avoir contracté mariage de leur abandonner tous ses biens, meubles et immeubles présens et avenirs qui pourroient lui appartenir en cette isle.*[3]

From other sources, moreover, come further clues to the paternity of the children, which indicate that some but not all the offspring of Brigitte freed by Pitois were his own. For when Brigitte, the slave above mentioned, went on to marry Jean Baptiste, a 'libre', the couple declared as their children, François, born in 1775, Marie Jeanne in 1776, Guillematte, and Adelaide, born in 1778 and 1780 respectively. At the time of the wedding, in 1780, Brigitte had already been enfranchised by Jean Pitois who declared his authorisation for her marriage. Brigitte's husband was described in the civil status register as a 'natif de Chandernagor originaire portugais venu en ce pays libre en 1773 ou 1774 actuellement pêcheur aux Quatre Cocos' [4].

It seems likely that only Vincent and Françoise, the two oldest offspring of Brigitte, were the children of Pitois. In fact when Françoise herself married a Frenchman, Romain Ferdinand Marnier 'ancien appointé au Régiment de l'Isle de France, maître serrurier demeurant à la Rivière Sèche', and a native of Brie in France, in 1792, she was described as a 'créole affranchie de Jean Pitois dit Prosper, fille adoptive de Jean

Baptiste Chandernagor noir libre et fille naturelle de Brigitte négresse malgache aussi affranchie du dit Pitois native de cette paroisse d'autre part'. The biological father of Françoise was not mentioned, but the likelihood of her half-French status is confirmed by her marriage to a Frenchman. Finally, a 'Vincent Pitois dit St Prosper' is listed as a free Creole aged 23 in the 1776 Census. He was in the 'milice noire' and resided at Rempart; his relationship to the family is unclear as he seems to be considerably older than the other children.[5]

It was in fact a common practice for the White fathers of Creole children to place them in military service, as a way of keeping them out of slavery. In the case of Quintin Fortuné, his free status did not, however, survive the taking over of the Isle of France by the British. His position was taken up by his patron, Marcenay, who petitioned the Queen's Commissioner on his behalf in 1826, explaining,

> *A young creole, son of a European by a negress, was, according to usage, given to the French Government for the purpose of being enrolled in the military service. Free himself, he was actually serving in a free corps at the taking of the colony. The Corps in which he served, was disbanded, after that event, by Governor Farquhar, he was notwithstanding, soon after taken, and sold as a slave.*

Upon investigation it was found that Fortuné's father was a surgeon named Quintin, and the child of his Indian female slave. When the boy was 15 years of age, his father wanted to enfranchise him, 'mais ses moyens pécuniaires ne lui permettant pas de le faire, il en fit la donation au Gouvernement Français, qui levait alors un corps militaire d'hommes de couleur libres, pour servir à la défense de cette île ... ce qui donna à l'affranchi du gouvernement l'état civil'. Quintin died without leaving a will so that the mother and the boy's siblings remained legally the slaves of the surgeon. They were put on sale together with the other goods of Quintin. After the conquest, Fortuné was also seized, 'et conduit chez l'agent de la curatelle qui le fit remettre en vente publique'.[6] With the best will in the world, then, it was not always easy for the White fathers of such children to free their enslaved families.

Louis Vigoureux was one of those few who, whilst securing the future, in his will, of his natural children, recognised them as products of his relationships with Coloured women. In his last testament, dated 22 December 1745, he made provision for his unborn child, whom his Chinese servant Pauline was expecting, in the form of a maintenance payment which would last until adulthood. He also expressed the desire to free the woman along with his unborn child and Gratia, another Chinese slave. In case the French Admiralty (which controlled enfranchisement procedures) failed to accede to this request, he mentioned that Pauline should marry Joseph, a free man. This was an alternative means of ultimately ensuring her freedom and that of the infant. His last testament states clearly that the signatory

> *a declaré avoir eu avec la nommée Francisca dies de Santo portugaise de nation et libre demeurante en cette isle et estant à son service, un enfant naturel nommé Nicolas âgé de six mois ou environ baptisé à l'église, paroisse de St Louis de cette île.*

He also recognised a second natural son, Jacques, by Francisca, and proposed to provide for them until they should reach adulthood, by settling 'deux mil livres' in 'rentes ou pension alimentaire' on them. For Francisca, meanwhile, he offered: 'la somme de sept cent piastres effective en argent blanc une fois payée, en outre une négresse esclave qui est celle qui la sert actuellement, nommée Maria'. However, this bequest was made on condition that Francisca quit the colony and leave her children behind! This was expressed in no uncertain terms by Vigoureux, who required that she:

> *sortir de cette isle pour passer soit à Mozambique soit à Goa qu'elle ne puisse sous quelques prétextes que ce puisse estre emmener avec elle les deux enfants qu'elle a eu dud. testateur au contraire veut et entend qu'ils restent en cette isle à la disposition de son exécuteur testamentaire cy-après nommé le priant d'exécuter et faire exécuter cette condition, comme aussy veut et entend ledit testateur, que tant que ladite Francisca dies de Santo sera demeurante en cette isle qu'elle ne puisse recevoir aucune chose des sept cents piastres à elle cy-dessus léguées mais ... que la ditte somme pourra luy être remise au cas qu'elle repasse soit à Mozambique ou à Goa.*

Whatever might have been the reason for this stipulation, this clause of Louis Vigoureux's will underscores the cruelty which could persist in such relationships despite the intimacy which occurred. At the same time, his generosity to his Chinese slaves permitted them to acquire a higher status in the Isle of France. Some time later we find the free Chinese woman, Gratia, has become a slave owner herself when the baptism of the daughter of her Mozambican slave Marie is recorded. Gratia evidently also had a child of her own, as in 1778, the marriage of 'Jean Gabriel pêcheur fils majeur de Gratia libre de caste chinoise' with the daughter of another Malay immigrant was celebrated. The civil status records also indicate the presence of a Joseph Santo, described as a 'noir de manille libre'. He married a Creole Indian woman by whom he had a child in 1780, before losing his wife on 21 February 1781 when she was around 20 years old. Elsewhere, his presence is signalled at the marriage of his wife's brother in 1780 when his name is recorded as 'Jean Baptiste Houat, noir créole libre de Santo originaire de Manille'. Could this person be related to the hapless Francisca de Santo? [7]

When found, *in flagrante*, white colonists had no choice but to bow to circumstances and admit the existence of a relationship, proscribed or not. Thus when Simon Martin, a 'tonnelier', was raided by the police, investigating a case of theft, and 'il y fut trouvé une négresse dans son lit', Martin was obliged to concede the point, later stating: 'il luy vint habituellement une négresse nommée Angélique Madécasse esclave de M. de Chazal que comme elle lave fréquemment à la Grande Rivière il ne se souvient point si elle ay étoit le même soir ou non'.[8] The links between *petits blancs*, or white soldiers and artisans and coloured or slave women have been described in detail by Jumeer (1984) and were regularly deplored by colonial administrators of the Isle of France. Cossigny described the behaviour of the French soldiers, then without barracks, and their female companions, in most unfavourable terms:

> *Les soldats sans cazerne, éparpillés de toute part, ne songent qu'à se procurer les moyens de se saouler d'eau de vie et à débaucher toutes les négresses de la loge, tant celles des travaux, que celles qui servent dans les maisons, en quoy, certes, il trouve de leur part, soit de nuit, soit de jour, les plus heureuses dispositions.*[9]

The White artisans under his charge lived and worked with the slaves also employed on the fortifications, with predictable results. On 29 June 1754 Cossigny described a fight which broke out between 40 sailors from the *Centaur* and the White and Black workers occupied on the Ile des Tonneliers: 'au jour parut nombre de noirs et de négresses avec de fières taloches sur la tête et sur le bras, quelques uns avoient les yeux pochés des coups qu'ils avoient reçus'.[10]

Very often, the existence of relationships between White men and slave women was blamed on the latter. In 1788 an Ordinance was passed restricting the mobility of slaves, on the grounds that female slaves hired out by their masters to indivuals

> *commettent sous ce prétexte de plus grands désordres encore. Elles se livrent à un libertinage effronté et crapuleux qui corrompt les moeurs et ruine la santé d'un genre d'hommes utile et précieux à l'état, les gens de mer et les soldats. De pareils désordres portent atteinte aux moeurs, au repos public et à la propriété des habitans.*[11]

In other cases, the relationships, though much talked about, remain speculative. The Madagascan princess, Betia, who lived at the Isle of France, is a good example. Marie Elizabeth Sobobie Bety or Betia was the daughter of Ratsimilaho, the betsimisaraka king, who ruled a section of the east coast of Madagascar including St Mary's island. When he died in 1750 she became queen and continued her father's policy of negotiating the cession of St Mary's to the French East India Company. In 1751 she came to the Isle of France, travelling between that island and her native Madagascar on several occasions to help settle disputes between the Malagasies and the French. She was given a number of land concessions at Flacq and Plaines Wilhems, was baptised in 1775 and naturalised in 1780. She died in Vacoas on 14 October 1805. Among her executors were René Charles Le François de Grainville Forval and Lislet Geoffroy. She left a modest fortune and 23 slaves. It has been speculated that Betia was the mistress of more than one Frenchman, and even that 'Gosse, Forval et La Bigorne avaient été des époux de Betia'. H. Adolphe & R. d'Unienville have concluded that 'cette assertion n'est pas probable quoique ces personnes aient eu avec Betia des relations d'affaires et d'amitié' (DBM:

1022-4; Macmillan, 1910: 133-5). The census data indicate the presence of four children in her household, Louise, Esther, Auguste and Julien, all Creoles of Mauritius. In the 1776 Census two of them are described as the children of Julie, her niece. In 1788 they are listed as aged between 14 and 10 years. [12]

Despite the proscriptions against such relationships some European men did formalize their liaisons with women of colour and even their former slaves. In 1771 Pierre Dufour, a native of Brittany in France, married Marie Christine, described in the civil status register as a 'Bengaly negress' and his former slave. In 1775, Nicholas Chauveau, a carpenter from Lille, married Françoise Morel, the minor daughter of Jean Jacques Morel and of Pauline Palma, the latter described as a Chinese woman from Canton.[13] In 1778 abuses were declared to have crept into the Civil Status registers of the colony and an *arrêté* reminded the population that:

> *Il est encore dans l'ordre que les actes de baptêmes, mariages et sépultures des blancs ne soient pas confondus avec ceux des noirs; la distinction qui règne dans la société entre les premiers qui naissent d'une condition bien supérieure aux seconds qui sont destinés à supporter le joug de l'esclavage doit régner également dans la manière de constater l'état et l'existence des uns et des autres.*

In the following year, a second Ordinance declared: 'faisons deffenses à tous blancs, de quelque qualité et conditions qu'ils soient, de demeurer en cette ville, dans les lieux habités par les noirs, leur enjoignions d'en sortir dans un mois à compter du jour de la publication de notre présente ordonnance à peine de 500 livres d'amende'.[14] Despite what must have been difficult conditions for the White spouses and partners of 'libres', it seems clear that the authorities were fighting a losing battle against the aspirations of a growing Coloured population which was daily extending its social and economic ties with the White colonists.

Social relationships between White men and Coloured women inevitably strengthened the economic status of the 'libre' class through property and bequests passed on to the wives or partners of such colonists. Allen (1983) has charted the rise of economic power of free women of

Colour and through them to their 'libre' husbands from the Isle of France and on into the 19th century. Economic relationships of many kinds also existed between White colonists and free men of Colour, whether their offspring, or through work relationships. The *arrêts civils* of the Conseil Supérieur of the Isle of France attest to the extensiveness of such economic ties, and to the prosperity of members of the coloured community. Thus, Jean de Silva, a 'noir libre' hired out his slaves to Sieur Haltet, and Sieur Gerville was indebted for the sum of 6,815 livres to Baptiste Bangard, a Malabar carpenter.[15]

Relationships between Whites and Coloureds during the French Revolution

During the Revolution, further such unions were legitimised and some members of the White population of the Isle of France, seemed disposed to emancipate the Coloured community from juridical discrimination. In

May 1791, Louis Monneron, in France, aligned himself with the Amis de Noirs, noting that the *mulâtres* and free Blacks in the Isle de France awaited 'les décisions de la Mère Patrie au milieu de la bonne volonté des blancs'. Back in the Isle of France, the Assemblée Coloniale voted political equality between White and Coloured citizens in May 1791 and on 24 pluviose An V or 12 February 1797, 'la liberté des dispositions gratuites entre tous les citoyens libres' (d'Unienville, 1979:37). Nagapen comments:

> *Les colons avaient accueilli dans l'allégresse le changement de régime causé par la Révolution. Puis, ils avaient apprécié la valeur démocratique du gouvernement local et de l'administration municipale. De plus, ils toléraient la proclamation purement théorique - somme toute, assez platonique - de l'égalité des blancs et des gens de couleur libres. Mais pas plus loin!* (Nagapen, 1996: 47)

Examples of the unions legitimised after 1789 can be easily found in civil status documents: in thermidor, year 2 of the Revolution, Pierre Lamargue of Charente married Françoise, the daughter of Francisque Thiampa, an Indian, and Thérèse, a Creole. In so doing, they legitimated their three children born in 1783, 1785 and 1788. In the same year, Joseph Quirin, a native of Sarre, married Jeanne, a freed Indian woman, the latter was 55 years old at the time. Both of these couples were no doubt taking advantage of the relaxed laws to formalise partnerships of a long standing nature. Marriages also took place between ex-slaves and Whites; thus in Year 4, Thomas Druce, a 43 year old Irish mechanic, married Julie, a 'native of Bengal', also his freed slave. She was 24 years old. In the same year, Angélique, a freed Indian woman, married her two 'créole mulâtresse' daughters (an implicit reference to her own relationship with a White man) to two French sailors from the ship *La Cibelle*. These marriages between White men and free Coloured women or ex-slaves are a testimony to the liberalization of relationships during the revolutionary period. It was also presumably less onerous for Whites to acknowledge their natural offspring as René André Oury did in 1791 when his child by Rosalie, Creole libre was baptised: 'Oury, négociant au port a reconnu l'enfant et s'est dit le père naturel'.[16]

With the return of Decaen, however, a step backwards was taken. His *arrêté* of 3 pluviose An XII (24 January 1804) re-established the laws of 1724; then by an *arrêté* of 19 brumaire An XIII (10 November 1804) he published an enfranchisement code which reintroduced the intermediary stage of the pre-Revolutionary years. On 1 brumaire An XIV (23 October 1805) the civil code was divided into separate legal systems: a law for Whites, for Coloureds and for slaves. According to this law, Whites could not adopt a freedman or bequeath property in his favour. The Coloured person's civil status was listed in the same registers as that of slaves and the owner who gave him/her freedom, retained a right to oppose his/her marriage. Property could not be disposed of between these two groups. (d'Unienville, 1979b: 37). As Nagapen describes it: 'Or, sous le Consulat, sur injonction de Paris, sans vergogne, le gouverneur Decaen fit table rase des décisions révolutionnaires sur ce chapître'. (Nagapen, 1996: 49). Moutou notes that the Code Decaen 'fut reçu comme un crime par toute la population de couleur' (Moutou, 1996: 140).

The intimacy of Whites and free Coloureds was once again questioned by the state, and numerous infringements of the law brought to the attention of the authorities. Etienne Carré, a native of Champagne who had arrived in the Isle of France as a soldier from the Pondicherry regiment in 1783 aboard *Le Barbeau*, was prosecuted in 1806 for the employment of Blacks to purchase stolen articles which he then sold on in a shop which he ran with his female partner. Asked his means of subsistence since his discharge from the army in 1791, he replied that Zaire Noripoint, the free Black woman with whom he lived, gave him 30 *piastres* per month. However, Michel, a 'noir mozambique', testified that 'tous les noirs lui portent quelque chose pour vendre ... il a entendu dire que Carré achetait du manioc et ce que les noirs pouvaient avoir'. Another member of the White population whose conduct aroused the suspicion of the Commandant of Savanne was Fedé, who arrived in An 11. His profession was 'maître d'hôtel', but on his arrival he took employ as a 'marchand colporteur'. He left the job and having no means of subsistence was reported to have 's'est mis au crochet d'une négresse libre'. [17] When Hipolite Dumoulin assaulted Aquel, a bourgeois, who was trying to defend Suzanne, 'négresse libre', from the former's aggression, an investigation into his case concluded that Dumoulin was a 'dissipateur et libertin ... un homme dangereux pour la colonie ... cet homme est arrivé il y a environ 3 ans sur un navire hambourgeois... depuis il a mérité l'animadversion particulière de la police'. It was decided that he should be embarked on *Le Charles Maurice*, to return him to France. In An 13 another dangerous character was recommended for ejection from the district of Grand Port, for various misdemeanours, which included excessive familiarity with Blacks:

> *Nous avons un citoyen nommé Louis Pommier, jeune homme qui a été matelot, qui est sans feu n'y lieu, courant d'une maison dans une autre, montrant à des petits noirs à lire, c'est un sujet dangereux, ... J'attends vos ordres, pour le faire conduire au port, pour débarrasser le quartier d'un être pareil.*

The lifestyle of promiscuous association with Blacks which these cases reveal was certainly common of *petits blancs* during this period. When respectable Whites took up with Blacks, however, sensibilities were immediately raised. Madame Latour conspired with Sieur Bigaignon to have her 18 year old son declared a vagabond and 'de le faire mettre en prison à la géôle après lui avoir lavé la tête' because 'il s'est mis dans la tette qu'il était riche, il ne veut plus rien faire', she suspected 'qu'il a une négresse'.[18]

Coloured men and women whose contacts with slaves aroused attention could equally become the object of investigation. Nina, a freed woman, was accused of having participated in a supper at a slave's house in the absence of the owner at which some damage occurred, resulting in an injunction to her 'd'être plus circonspecte à l'avenir et ne plus fréquenter des négresses esclaves'. In 1807, the Commissaire Civil of Savanne reported on Mignot, born at Isle Bonaparte, a coloured man 28 years old, who had appeared in the district two years earlier 'debarqué d'un corsaire, exerçant la profession de cordonnier; il a travaillé quelque temps dans l'atelier de Laingetas cordonnier blanc du quartier... sa mauvaise conduite, ne lui permettant pas de se fixer nulle part, il est devenu vagabond... se retirant fort souvent dans les camps des noirs sur les grands établissements... pour y vivre de leurs rapines'. A second letter confirmed that the estate owners suspected him of being involved in an armed robbery on one of their properties in the company of six Blacks. He was described as 'jeune vigoureux, d'une jolie tournure et d'un teint qui souvent le fait prendre pour un blanc'.[19] It was decided that the district would be well rid of him also. Mignot's case reveals the facility with which young light-skinned men could pass from the society of the White artisans to that of the Black slaves, participating in the sub-economy of the slaves and acting as a conduit whilst living outside the norms of White society.

The newly frustrated aspirations of the freed Coloured community created considerable tensions among Whites during this period. In 1809 Sieur La Carrière brought a case against 'trois mulâtres qu'il a accusé d'avoir insulté toute sa famille devant la porte de sa maison par les propos les plus révoltans', and in An 12 Constant Laroche, convicted of insulting 'Gillard, blanc sexagénaire', was given one month's prison and a fine 'avec injonction d'être à l'avenir plus circonspect et respectueux envers les blancs'. However, when a White officer in the 'marine marchande' was convicted of having 'frappé la négresse Chardavoine dans sa maison et pendant la nuit', having already been warned by the police not to go to her house or to insult her, he was given a 15 day prison sentence and a large fine.[20] Citizens of colour were not destitute of rights even under the Empire.

In fact, free Coloureds regularly contested the non-payment of bequests and claimed money from their former enfranchisers, at a time when the process of acquiring freedom had been subjected to successive restrictions, which created a further source of tension. Thus in 1808 Sinanande, 'femme libre de Madagascar' contested the will of Daniel Yekell, and in 1809 Rosalie, 'affranchie et tutrice de sa fille mineure' of Castaing, demanded from his executors the sums bequeathed to her. Marie Jeanne 'femme de couleur' demanded from her enfranchiser himself, Chenard, the 3,000 *piastres* he had promised her in the act of liberty.[21] Ultimately, however, the restitution of those claims to equality promised by the Revolution to the Coloured community was condemned to await the slow progress of British legislation following the conquest of the Isle of France. Slaves, for their part, continued to be held to strict laws requiring them to show respect for their social betters. In An 12 'un esclave prévenu d'avoir donné un soufflet à un blanc' was condemned 'au fouet, à la marque, à l'exposition 3 dimanches et aux galères à perpétuité'. A female slave was luckier, 'prévenue d'injures graves et de voyes de fait envers une femme de la population blanche', her sentence was relatively light - she was given 'une année de fers, attendu les circonstances atténuantes du délit'. Presumably she had been sorely tried by her mistress! [22]

Inter-Ethnic Relationships in the 'Libre' and Slave Communities

As the above cases demonstrate, over the course of the 18th century many Indian, African and Creole women became independent property-owners, often following liaisons with colonists who liberated them if they were not already free and bequeathed goods and slaves to them. Their status enabled them to intermarry with the free Malabar community, imported as artisans: Narcisse Sinappa and Jean Louis Moutou both married Creole women of West African descent. In Sinappa's case, however, he was a 35 year old Indian-born slave and freed for his marriage with the 45 year old widow Marie Louise, herself the daughter of a free *Guinée* couple, perhaps indicating that considerations of property and status were also involved in the match. These free men of colour willingly adopted the children which their wives had previously conceived with the White owners who enfranchised them. J. Crousse, a native of India who arrived in the Isle of France in 1750, married Thérèse, a Malagasy, 19 years his junior. By 1788 he was already a grandfather, having had 7 children, his eldest daughter, then aged 19, was herself the mother of two daughters. It is likely that some of the children recensed by Crousse were adopted offspring. The daughters of these relationships between White colonists and slave women, once free and integrated into the 'libre' population could themselves aspire to cohabit with the lower ranks of White society, and even to marry such partners during the Revolutionary years. On 28 May 1792, Marie Jeanne, described as 'créole libre fille adoptive de Jean Baptiste Crousse noir Indien libre et fille naturelle de Thérèse négresse Malgache affranchie de François Grange de cette paroisse d'autre part', married a White. Her husband, Christian Frédéric Hom was recorded as 'ancien soldat au régiment de l'île de France, tailleur d'habit, natif de Steilein en Prusse fils majeur de défunt Jean Ephrem Hom et de Marie Hubers demeurant aux Cent Gaulettes paroisse Notre Dame de Grand Port'. [23]

There were also numerous inter-regional marriages within the Indian or Malabar community between such freed slave women and 'libre' men: Thomé Naletamby, a free Malabar from Negapatam and a peon in the service of the Port Louis police, married Catherine Papouty, a freed Bengali slave. This trend was even more marked among Creole Malabars (ie Malabars born in the Isle of France) like Denys, an apprentice carpenter, who married a Bengali, Marie Louise, freed with her son for the wedding by her owner, Roquefort. When Roquefort ceded her to Denys, the son of free Indians, he was acknowledging and helping to legitimise a relationship which had begun when Marie Louise was still his slave. European owners frequently gave up their women slaves for such unions, even, when as we have seen, the women were their former mistresses. Marie, the Bengali slave of a European merchant, was expressly given up by her owner and confided to Félicien Jérôme, a free Indian from Karaikal, in order for her to contract marriage with the latter. In many cases, free Malabars purchased female slaves of their own ethnic group, established relationships with, and later married them. When Josephine Franchine of Madras married Jean Louis Basile of Pondicherry, they formalised a relationship which had lasted more than eleven years, during which time she was freed by him and bore him six children.[24]

The nature of such interactions between free Malabars and ex-slaves demonstrates the fluid character of the community, and the possibility of social mobility, particularly for female slaves. The connotations of the state of servility for such women must have been very different than for a *noir de pioche*, who was nevertheless their equal before the law, and demonstrate the difficulty of defining the relative positions of slave and free in 18th century colonial society. This data also provide some insights into the character of the free Indian community in the Isle of France and its place within the social hierarchy. Despite some opposition to the principle of allowing Hindu Malabars to own slaves in a Catholic state, this was over-ruled, revealing once again, the divergence between policy and practice in a colony where non Christian inhabitants had attained powerful and respected positions. The role of free Indians as slave-owners was necessarily ambiguous. Many members of the community owned significant numbers of slaves of differing ethnic groups. Catherine, a 29 year old Malagasy negress owned twelve slaves, at her Pamplemousses residence in 1776, whilst Bangard, a Creole residing in the Camp Malabar, was listed as owning nine slaves. In Port Louis alone, the 1776 census records that the 'libre' population possessed more than 300 slaves between them.[25] They became embroiled in disputes over their slaves just like any other owners. At the same time, there is ample evidence of lasting partnerships developing between them and their slaves, of their efforts to purchase kin and family out of slavery, and even of attempts made to introduce dependants under the status of slaves in order to settle them in the island (Jumeer: 230-1).

Female members of the Malabar community also entered into relationships with 'libre' Africans. In 1794, Pierre Maquin Azor 'libre par l'acquisition qu'il a fait de sa personne' and a native of Madagascar, married one of the legitimate children of Jean Baptiste 'libre de Chandernagore' and of Brigitte, the former slave of Pitois. The new bride was called Adelaide, and was presumably the daughter recognised at her parents' wedding as having been born of their union in 1778. Ascribed the 'caste' of her father rather than of her mother, she was recorded as a 'Bengali créolle de cette isle'. In Year 8 Julienne, another daughter of the same couple married the much older François, also 'natif de Madagascar'. The children of Brigitte were therefore establishing relationships across the ethnic spectrum, since, as we have seen, Adelaide's half-sister had married a White Frenchman. [26] Some Indian women married the African men who had purchased them as slaves: in 1778 Paul, a free Malagasy married his Bengali slave Suzanne, and recognised their two children. Another resident of Anse Courtois, Albert, a Mozambican employed as 'facteur de la poste établie pour l'intérieur de l'isle', also married a Bengali slave.[27]

The free African community integrated within it, like the Malabars, those individuals who, being the offspring of White men and African women, took the 'caste' of the mother, whilst retaining the privileged status which their half French status accorded them. Joseph Mayeur's situation suggests that he was one of this number. In Year 11 he was a 23 year old resident of Flacq, and described as 'né à Madagascar, arrivé en cette île en 1784 sur le vaisseau Hercule...confié par sa mère au citoyen Mayeur habitant de ce canton chez qui il est domicilié et qui est son protecteur,... fils naturel de la nommée Valahondibra demeurant à Madagascar'. One of the best known such cases is that of Lislet Geoffroy. When he married Marie Jeanne, a 'Créole Guinée', at Port Louis in May 1780 he was described as 'Jean Baptiste Créole de Bourbon Guinée libre connu sous le nom de Lislet piqueur sur les travaux du Roy, fils majeur de Marie Geneviève ditte Niama Guinée affranchie de Geoffroy habitant l'Isle de Bourbon'. In the same year another son of Niama, and therefore brother to Jean Baptiste, the 26 year old Louis, 'Caporal de Noirs Libres', died at a tragically early age. [28]

Again, like the Malabars, the African community of the Isle of France incorporated within it high status families whose heritage and identity were recognised through their appellations and their family units. Beti and Sensée were two such dominant Malagasy females; Lislet Geoffroy was one of several *Guinée* families. The presence of West Africans in the island dates from the early predominance of slaves from this part of Africa. The marriages in 1733 celebrated between Louis 'noir du Sénégal', and Pallas, a *Guinée* slave; and between Claude Rencontre, 'noir de Guinée', with Jeanne, 'femme yolof', are cases in point. Some retained a semblance of their African names such as Louis Feridiama 'noir yolof', or a tribal name as in the case of 'Mathurin Bambara noir du Sénégal'. A few of these names, like Dimba, have been maintained into present day Mauritius. Of course, numerous inter-regional marriages also occurred amongst Africans; thus in Thermidor Year 5, Jean César, described as a 'citoyen de couleur né à Madagascar', married Marie Cécile of Mozambique.[29]

Within the slave community itself, relationships between different ethnic groups was the norm. Only legitimated relationships are preserved in the civil status records: an early example occurred in 1729 when Laurence, a negress from the Malabar coast, is listed as having married a Malagasy. The permutations of marriages between slaves of the various 'castes' or 'nations' are too numerous to cite. The following table makes a case study of marriages contracted by enslaved or freed individuals originating from the subcontinent of India (and whose ethnic status would have been variously recorded as 'malabar', 'telinga', 'coringhee', 'bengaly' or 'indien') with partners whose ethnic status is also given. The results reveal that while intra-nation marriage was the most common partner choice, it was not unusual for women of Indian origin to marry African men, whilst marriages between Indian men and African women also occurred. It should be noted that these figures probably vastly underestimate the number of inter-ethnic slave relationships which occurred, both because they take no account of non-formalised unions and secondly because the numerous marriages between Indians and Creoles, ie persons born in Mauritius - where ethnic origin is not explicitly stated - have not been listed here.

Marriages involving Indian Slaves by Ethnic Group in the Isle of France, 1729-1810

Ethnic Status of Couple	No. of Marriages
Male Indian with Female Indian	73
Male Indian with Female Malagasy	6
Male Indian with Female Mozambican	1
Male Indian with Female Other	6
Female Indian with Male Malagasy	33
Female Indian with Male Mozambican	13
Female Indian with Male Other	6
Total Number of Marriages	128

NB The 'Other' category includes slaves belonging to minority nations such as Malay, Juda or Guinée.
SOURCE: ANOM Etat Civil Records, 1729-1810

It has been suggested by some historians that inter-ethnic slave marriage was more a reflection of the owner's whim than of the slave's selection of a spouse, since the racial antipathy which existed on the part of Indians towards Africans would not have predisposed such unions (Napal: p 39-40; Milbert: 181-82; Toussaint, 1972: 170). The state of servility must have acted as a constraint on free choice of partner, but the notion that inter-ethnic relationships were forced rather than voluntary, belies the evidence that many such marriages were also contracted by freed slaves and by 'libres'. Contemporary sources suggest, furthermore, that notions of superiority were not confined to Indians. Bouvet, writing in 1755, noted that the Malagasys considered themselves a cut above the *lascars* who manned the ships sent to bring them to servitude. He expressed the fear that 'les noirs de Madagascar qui sont entreprenants et qui méprisent les Indiens ne causent des révoltes dans ces bâtiments'.[30]

The racial stereotypes current in the Isle of France have nevertheless persuaded Filliot that Indian slaves were an 'elite' and has led Dupon to describe them as 'une aristocratie du travail minoritaire mais effective de domestiques et d'artisans' (Filliot: 175; Dupon: 1055). One measure of the validity of the notion would be to determine that Indian slaves were more valuable than other ethnic groups. In fact slave price data from the Isle of France offers no concrete evidence of this (Carter, 1990: 242-3). Were Indians employed in significantly different occupations, then? Again employment figures compiled for slaves of all ethnic groups owned by the French East India Company demonstrate that by and large Indians performed the same work as African slaves. The first slave registration of British Mauritius in 1817, equally reveals that the most important occupation of Indian slaves - both men and women - was that of field hand, or '*pioche*' (Carter, 1990: 243-5). Domestic servants accounted for sizeable proportions of slaves of all ethnic groups, and on the basis of this data, it is not plausible to conclude that ethnicity was an important factor in defining the position, privileged or not, which a slave might occupy. It is misleading to elevate one racial category to the status of an elite within the servile population on the strength of contemporary observations alone. The historical evidence suggests that the proximity in the Isle of France of diverse ethnic groups encouraged inter-ethnic ties rather than the entrenchment of hierarchical communal divisions which were woven into state policy, but only ineffectually imposed from above.

The Creolization Process: Some Case Studies

The Lettres Patentes of 1723 required that slaves be instructed in the Catholic religion and large numbers of adult slaves were baptized, as were their creole offspring. The civil status data seems to reflect the efficacy of the proselytization of slaves in the 18th century. Many slaves were Muslims or Hindus at the time of their arrival in the Isle of France. In some cases, as where names reveal a religious identity, we can trace the apparent rapidity of absorption into a Catholic Creole society. Uzirmahmod and Koki from Calcutta were Muslim slaves. Their son was named Hector and married Sophie, a native of 'Coringhee', after they had both been freed by their owner, Christophe Martin. Their eight year old daughter also became free. Within one generation then, the child of Muslim slaves was baptised and married a baptised woman who was probably a Telegu in origin. When Thérèse married Tacambo of Bengal in 1793, it is revealed that her parents were named Rama and Moutama, of Pondicherry. Tacambo and Thérèse were both the freed slaves of Antoinette. They probably shared a common Hindu origin. By the mid 18th century the births of Creole grandchildren of Indian slaves are being recorded, and by this third generation, the traces of Indian origin become increasingly difficult to ascertain. Indian and particularly Hindu/Moslem nomenclature was more likely to survive where the slave owners were themselves of Indian origin. Thus in 1775 Moutou, a free Malabar, reported the death of his 80 year old Malabar slave Rama.

However, a Christian first name did not necessarily indicate a religious conversion. Many slaves and free Coloureds continued to practise their religions despite taking new names. Thus Assoury, described as a 'lascard sarangue', married a woman named Louise, but in his letter requesting permission for his wedding from the 'chefs de cette isle' dated 13 November 1781, he noted that Louise was a 'négresse libre de sa caste', suggesting a shared ethnic origin. Their child was baptised Louis. Another 'sarangue des lascards', Pierre Abraham, also known as Absoul, was administered 'les sacremens de pénitence et d'extrême onction' on his deathbed in 1778. Pierre's wife, Suzanne Rosalie, was, like himself, a 'lascard libre'. Baptised Indians with Catholic names were known in some cases to continue to practice their Hindu or Muslim faith, so that their Christianity was effectively for public consumption only (Jumeer p 459-60). Indians adapted to the prevailing ethos by maintaining a religious identity separate from, but within, the Catholic state. Even a 'prêtre lascar' like Abdoul Ramen, married a baptised ex-slave named Jeanne 'dite Babou' in 1806.[31]

Other slaves and free Indians, particularly those brought from the French *comptoirs* in India (Chandernagore in Bengal, Pondicherry, Mahé, Yanum and Karraikal in the South) or from Portuguese Goa were already Catholics and to some extent inducted into European culture. South Indian Catholic origins can be ascertained from the name as in the case of the marriage celebrated in 1734 between Xavier Chabrymoutou and Rose, slaves of Coignart. The relationship between Catholic Malabars from the French settlements and South Indian Hindu traders is an interesting one. It seems likely that the wealth and influence of both groups, together with a shared ethnicity, increased the desirability of intermarriage. Certainly apparently non-Christian Indians like Sinnatamby Marimoutou Chety who married a Creole Christian in 1808, were able to establish close links with the Catholic Coloured community. [32] On the other hand, Jumeer cites evidence of hostility between Hindu and Catholic factions within the Malabar community (p. 253-7, 311-2). The appointment of Denis Pitchen as head of the Malabars in 1784 may equally be seen as an attempt by the state to subvert the power of the Hindu faction by the appointment of an Indo-Catholic. The Catholic fervour of some Malabars - they petitioned for a chapel to be built in the Camp des Malabars, for example - may have aggravated tensions between the two groups. In general, however, the evidence suggests that many Malabars effectively imbued Christian religious observances at baptisms and marriages in the Isle of France, with Tamil rites and traditions. Indian dress (turbans and saris) continued to be worn, and some Hindu practices observed in private (Nagapen, 1987: 36-7; Gerbeau, p.9-10; Sooriamoorthy, p. 40).

When 15 citizens petitioned the Colonial Assembly in 1793, protesting about the 'costume des citoyens de couleur d'origine indienne,' the Colonial Assembly not only refused to intervene but legislated some time later enabling Indians in the 'corps des chasseurs de la Garde Nationale' to maintain their dress and customs: 'l'Assemblée permet aux Malabars de conserver leurs toques, mais si leur nombre le comporte ils seront tems de former des compagnies séparées afin de ne pas blesser l'uniformité'. Similarly when Le Normand articulated the fears of some colonists regarding the size of the Malabar community by demanding 'un règlement qui distingue les malabars et les lascars, qu'on les soumette à une exacte surveillance et qu'on prenne des mesures pour arrêter la trop grande augmentation de ces castes dans la colonie' the Assembly refused to debate the motion (d'Unienville, 1982: 59). The Malabars also took care to protect their position in society by adopting some tenets of the colonising power whilst maintaining their own traditions.

Minority ethnic groups within the Isle of France society were more likely to become 'creolized', through constant intermarriage with other groups. This was particularly the case for the small Malay/Chinese community. We have already seen that Pauline Palma, herself the wife of a White, married her daughter to another Frenchman. Other ethnic 'Chinese' married Indians and Africans leading to the creation of Sino-Indian and Sino-African sub groups, usually Catholicised, and who ultimately merged into the larger Creole population. The presence of this population group dates from the early French period: Mahé de Labourdonnais himself owned a Chinese slave named Simon, a carpenter by trade. Louis Vigoureux, as noted above, left a will in favour of his female Chinese slaves Pauline and Gracia, and at least two systematic importations were made of Chinese by the Comte d'Estaing in 1760 and by Charles de Constant in 1783 (Ng, 1996: 3).

The free and slave Malays married a range of ethnic groups: Antoine, 'noir malais' married Marie, a Bengalie. Domingue of Macao, a freed Chinese, son of Chinese slaves, married Rita from Mozambique, a slave sold to him for the marriage. Their daughter, Jeanne, in turn married, at the age of 24, a freed Malagasy. Within the slave population Mercure, a

Malagasy, married Camille, a Malay, in 1775. Matthieu, born at Flacq in 1770, was the son of François, a Creole Malagasy, and Jacqueline, a Malay, both slaves. During the Revolution, the civil status registers record that Geneviève, a Malay woman, married Pierre Moutou, who was employed as a clerk. This was evidently a relatively high status marriage as the powerful Pitchen family, including J.D. Pitchen and P.P. Pitchen who was head of the government pions, attended the wedding, and suggests that Geneviève was integrated into the Malabar community. At the time of the marriage the couple legitimated their three children. [33] However, some Chinese did marry others of a similar ethnic background as the marriage of Gratia's son, described above, demonstrates.

Negotiating a path though the maze of inter-ethnic relationships which characterised Isle of France society is complicated further by the inaccuracies of 'caste' and 'nation' data. One must be wary of defining individuals too narrowly. It is not always possible, for example, to attribute the status Malay/Chinese to a South East Asian or Chinese origin. Cases occur in census and civil status records where individuals born in Macao are described as Indians. Region of origin data is similarly haphazard. Periman is described in some records as being from the Coromandel coast, and elsewhere as having been born in Bombay. Persons of mixed origin created particular problems for the authorities whose task it was to define persons according to their rank. Some individuals were already of mixed origin on their arrival in Isle of France: when Antoine married the freed Bengali woman Véronique, he was described as a 'noir libre mistiche de Trinquebard, arrivé sur le vaisseau du roi Loriston en qualité de matelot'. When Marie Jeanne, a Bengali, died in 1790, the register carefully noted that she had been born in 1778 at Dacca where she had been baptised and that her mother 's'est mariée 4 ans après la naissance dudit enfant au nommé Antoine Pitre Européen Blanc'. These carefully recorded details suggest the importance, until death, to such individuals and their families of the particular circumstances of their birth. *Mulâtres* (offspring of a white/coloured relationship) would be identified as such, but might also take the caste of the mother. Thus Veuve Latour's female slave Catherine was described as a 'créole mulâtre caste mozambique' . If the paternity of the child was uncertain, the alternative appellations would both be entered in the civil status register, so that when François Mathurin was born in Pamplemousses on 20 March 1767, he was listed as 'négrillon ou mulâtre, fils naturel de Charlotte créole Mozambique esclave de Herman'. The status of Hyacinthe is even more confusing, because she was described as 'négresse créole sang mêlé caste Mozambique'. Ultimately, as these data reveal, attempts to enumerate individuals according to racial classifications were doomed to failure and practically impossible for the historian to decipher. [34]

Some appellations defy characterisation. What does one make of the slave Java Vaja, described as a 'mozambique Java' of complexion 'cuivré'? And what about the status of Antoine Janvier, 'noir créol européen'? When he married in 1790 he was described as a 'charcutier, natif du Gudelle, évêché de Vannes, province de Bretagne, fils majeur de Joseph Janvier et Marie Françoise Indiens libres de cette paroisse'. How his Indian parents came to be in France when he was born, is another as yet untold story from the colourful past of the Isle of France. The ethnic status of Pierre Delair is even more confusing . In 1793 his death was recorded in the following words 'le nommé Pierre Marie Delair mulâtre, natif de Bretagne, âgé d'environ 22 ans fils de Théodore Delair noir et de Marie Vaillant'. His *mulâtre* status suggests that he must have had one White parent, perhaps his mother. [35] The attribution of a 'libre' status can only be gleaned from the definition of an individual as such in the Civil Status registers, since confusion over labels and designations is similarly great. Portuguese was a caste attributed to the Coloured community as seen above. However, when Louis Le Vaillant, corsair, married in Port Louis on 24 November 1794 a 16 year old Portuguese girl born in Macao, Roza Ombelina de Silva Monterro, he may well have been marrying another European (DBM: 1289). These difficulties in themselves reveal the absurdity and the impossibility of reconciling life in a small island society with the colonial precepts of dividing and classifying the population.

The White colonists of the Isle of France intermixed with Libres and slaves at different levels. *Negocians*, or *habitans* might have unacknowledged relationships with women from these groups, *marchands* and *ouvriers* were more likely to intermarry with them. The libre population came closest to bridging the social divide with *petits blancs* during the Revolutionary years, but the social history of the Isle of France reveals that juridical proscription could never hope to prevent the blurring of such boundaries, whilst racial classification could never keep pace with the complexity and diversity of the burgeoning population and their inter-relationships.

References

1. ANOM EC Port Louis 6 juillet 1732, and no 25, Port Bourbon, 1774-1794. 'Mistiche' seems to have been another term used to ascribe a mixed-race status, see for example EC Port Louis 11 avril 1772; ANOM EC Port Louis 22 déc 1771; 6 juin 1774; 10 avril 1781.
2. ANOM G2/218 Arrêts Civils du Conseil Supérieur, 15 juin 1785.
3. MA OA 75 Registre pour servir à l'enregistrement des actes de liberté accordée à des esclaves, 1768-1785.
4. ANOM EC No 7 Flacq, 6 juin 1780.
5. ANOM EC no 8 Flacq 28 may 1792; G1/473 Recensement de 1776;
6. PRO CO 415/4 Letter of L.F. Marcenay, 6 déc. 1826.
7. MA NA 8/3C Testament de Louis Vigoureux, 22 déc.1745, quoted in Ng, 1996: 2; ANOM EC Port Louis 7 mai 1777; no 37 Port Louis 17 fév 1778; Port Louis 19 juillet , 12 août 1780.
8. MA G2/222 Greffes, 27 sept. 1780
9. ANOM DFC Carton 10 Mémoire no 49, Journal de Cossigny, 14 déc. 1753.
10. ANOM DFC Carton 10 Mémoire no 52, Journal de Cossigny, 30 juin 1754.
11. G2/224 Ordonnance, 30 juin 1788.
12. G1/473 Recensement général de l'Isle de France, 1776; G1/474, 1780
13. ANOM EC Moka 1771, Port Louis, 22 juin 1775.
14. ANOM G2/224 Ordonnances et Réglements, arrêtés 18 nov. 1778 et 24 déc. 1779.
15 ANOM G2/217 Arrêts civils du Conseil Supérieur, 17 mai 1781; and G2/223 23 oct. 1785.

16. ANOM EC no 4 Flacq, 30 avril 1793; no 25 Port Bourbon, 29 thermidor An 2; Pamplemousses An 4 and Port Louis An 4; Port Louis 13 avril 1791.

17. ANOM G2/225 no 116 Pièces pour mandats d'arrêts, 1806 cases of Carré and Fedé.

18. Idem, cases of Dumoulin and Pommier, no 98, an 14 for that of Latour.

19. ANOM Greffes, 24 floréal An 12; G2/225 case of Mignot, 4 fév, and 2 mars 1807.

20. Idem, case of Sieurs La Carrière, no 16 7 jan 1809; Greffes, Germinal, An 12.

21. ANOM Greffes, Cour d'Appel, 1809-10, and Tribunal de 1ère Instance, 1806.

22. Idem and ANOM G2/226 Cour d'Appel, 1807.

23. ANOM EC G1/476 Recensement de 1788; EC MOKA 7 sep 1806; ANOM EC no 8 Flacq 28 mai 1792.

24. ANOM EC 50 Port Louis, 12 juin, 6 nov and 25 nov 1780.

25. ANOM EC G1/473 Recensement de 1776.

26. ANOM EC Flacq 16 mars 1794; no.25 Port Bourbon 16 Brumaire an 8.

27. ANOM EC no 37 Port Louis 19 jan 1778; 31 août 1778

28. ANOM EC Reg no.6: Flacq 4 pluviôse an 11; Port Louis 3 mai 1780, 3 oct 1780. Niama was said to be the daughter of a king of the Galam tribe, caught up in a razzia, and sold as a slave at the age of 9. Her son Lislet Geoffroy, engineer and cartographer, died in 1836, aged 70. A Nagapen, *L'Express*, 18 July 1988.

29. ANOM EC Port Louis 6 jan, 11 avril, 7 nov, 14 déc. 1733; EC no 4 Flacq, 30 avril 1793.

30. ANOM DFC Carton 11 Mémoire no 80, Bouvet aux Directeurs de la Co., 25 nov 1755.

31. ANOM G2/218 Arrêts Civils du Conseil Supérieur, 10 déc 1785; EC Port Louis 26 fév 1778; Port Louis, 1806.

32. ANOM EC no 46 Port Louis 26 mai 1808; Port Louis 11 sept 1777.

33. ANOM EC no 28 Port Louis, 1775 and 1778; EC Pamplemousses 13 oct 1789; EC no 54 Rivière du Rempart 1807-9; EC no 27 Port Louis 1775; EC no 1 Flacq 1770; EC 40 Port Louis.

34. ANOM EC no 14 Pamplemousses 15 mars, 20 mars et 20 déc. 1767; EC no 27, Port Bourbon, 1780-1792; EC Port Louis 1 sep 1790.

35. PRO T 71/568 Slave Registry of 1817; ANOM EC Port Louis 19 oct 1790; 21 mai 1793.

Whites, Creoles and Indians: Vignettes from a History of Mutual Dependence

Raymond d'Unienville

Whilst constraint and hierarchical social divisions are features of all colonial societies, it is not possible to construct and maintain a colony through sheer force and fear alone. Mauritius under French and British rule may have been peopled by many involuntary immigrants, yet its social history is replete with examples of mutual co-operation at times of political and economic crisis. The Isle of France could not have defended itself against the ever present threat of British attack without the services of slaves and free Blacks, whilst the financial crises and political developments of the late 19th and early 20th centuries were managed and steered by interest groups which were able to co-operate at crucial times despite in many instances representing conflicting ambitions. Whilst contestation and rebellion and its concomitant suppression is the more usual stuff of colonial narratives, this paper offers some insights into the many untold stories of individuals who developed personal relationships with those who employed or controlled them which triumphed over self-interest.

The Military Role of Slaves and Free Coloureds in the Isle of France

It is common knowledge that slaves and free artisans from Africa and Asia were crucial to the construction of a French settlement on the former Dutch possession of Mauritius. Their military role has been less well documented. During the 18th century, the Isle of France was frequently at war with one or more European powers, and its small garrison would not have been able to repel an attack without the assistance of the civilian population. Nagapen has documented the early use of Indian slaves in the military service of the embryonic colony: 'Labourdonnais had blazed the trail by enlisting Indian slaves in his army and on board his flotilla. His successors followed suit. Whenever threats of war loomed ahead, whether

on land or at sea, Indian slaves, especially those born on the island, were equipped with rifles. Thus when the English Admiral Boscawen threatened Pondicherry, they took part in Bouvet de Lozier's rescue expedition'(Nagapen, 1984:6). Writing in 1761, one colonial administrator described the success of Labourdonnais' expedition to Madras, which was all the more extraordinary because for 'plus de six ans on n'avait vu sortir aucun vaisseaux des ports de France, ni fait passer aucun soldat dans l'Inde'. The White, Creole, and Black slave force mustered by Labourdonnais from the Isle of France had thus been crucial, and it was reported that Mahé had recruited 'un grand nombre de noirs de la bonne espèce, des caffres de Guinée et de Mozambique, qu'il s'étoit occupé, pendant près de deux ans, à faire des soldats des uns, des autres des canonniers et gens propres à servir les vaisseaux'.[1]

From Labourdonnais' time onwards, slaves were regularly employed on cannon duty. In 1767 a defence plan for the island sent to France by Dumas, laid great stress on the role of slaves in any war involving the Isle of France:

> *Dès que les commandants des quartiers seront établis il sera fait dans toutes les habitations un choix parmy les noirs pour les exercer en service de l'artillerie et les plus sûrs d'entre eux tels que sont les créols seront exercés au fusil comme cela s'est pratiqué sans inconvénient dans ces colonies pendant les guerres précédentes... Le Noir est icy presque comme un paysan polonais attaché à la Glèbe et souvent content de son sort. Il y a généralement parlant plus d'humanité envers les esclaves qu'à St Domingue et à la Martinique. Tout noir créol se regarde comme citoyen et n'est pas humilié de l'infériorité de sa couleur. Cette espèce d'hommes a fait merveilles dans toutes les expéditions de M de la Bourdonnaye par terre et par mer, dans celles de M Dupleix et M Le Comte d'Estaing, et sur tous les vaisseaux de guerre ou armés en guerre où ils se sont trouvez devant l'ennemy depuis la fondation de la Colonie ... Un particulier possesseur de 8000 noirs en a fait dresser 500 depuis la dernière guerre aux exercices militaires et nous a donné la preuve par là de l'utilité d'une telle pratique. Nul établissement dans cette colonie n'a des noirs plus fidèles, mieux policés, plus soumis; l'honneur d'être armés ... fait parmi eux un objet d'émulation, car ces gens là ont aussy leur honneur à eux, il n'y a qu'à l'exciter et le diriger vers le bien de la chose publique.*

D'Estaing was convinced that the slaves of the Isle of France were more than a match for the native troops raised by the British in India. Writing in 1774 he described them as 'fort supérieurs aux cipayes qu'ils auroient à combattre, parce qu'ils sont susceptibles de bravoure et de fidélité'. To illustrate his point he quoted examples of courage and bravery of Creole

Blacks in a struggle with the English around the French fort of Papanooly in Sumatra, such as the statement of a wounded Black who insisted on remaining in the ranks, 'moy veux mourir comme un blanc'. D'Estaing added that no Blacks deserted to the Dutch as many Whites had done.[2]

When Souillac was Governor of the island, the cannon corps was increased to include 300 'noirs d'élite', destined to participate in the expedition to India, and divided into four companies of 25 Whites and 75 Blacks. Officers were appointed from among the slaves. The Isle of France at that time being well supplied with cloth following the capture of the *Osterley*, Souillac decided to provide the Blacks with a uniform. Article VII of the Ordinance he promulgated concerning the 'Détachement du corps de l'Artillerie qui doit passer dans l'Inde', stipulated

> *Tous les noirs porteront un gilet bleu, parements et collet rouge, un grand caleçon bleu; les caporaux porteront un double galon jaune sur chaque manche, et les appointés un seulement, et tous auront des casques.* (d'Unienville, 1979a: 53).

For the first time, slaves wore military uniform in the name of France. They boarded Suffren's ships on 30 November 1781, 550 in number, embarked in groups on each of the 11 vessels, and adding to the glamour of the occasion: 'En ces temps-là le spectacle était ... haut en couleurs, magnifique par ce goût de parader qui caractérisait autant les hommes que les femmes. D'abord les noirs, dans leurs uniformes flambant neuf, cinquante par vaisseau' (d'Unienville, 1979a: 66). Despite the remoteness of the campaign, these slaves from the Isle of France, were, in a small way, helping to contribute to the success of American Independence.

When the coastal batteries were periodically upgraded at times of war, Indians worked alongside Whites in their restoration. In May 1793 the intelligence of war with Austria was received at the Isle of France, and the fear of conflict with England, Holland and Spain was mooted. Accordingly on 11 September 1793, the Chief Engineer asked for 'une exemption de service de la Garde Nationale pour les commis apareilleurs Blancs, Malabards, chargés de la conduite des travaux relatifs à la défense de la colonie'.[3] In August, following Malartic's directions, slaves between

Private, Chasseurs coloniaux, 1803-10

the age of 15 to 50 were ordered to undertake 2 days of work at the fortifications.[4] Jocet established a project entitled 'noirs à fournir aux fortifications' which requested citizens of thc Isle of France 'qui reconnaîtront en quelques uns de leurs noirs assez de fidélitéet de bravoure pour concourir à servir la République dans la défense de la colonie' to register them at their local Municipality for the 'Comité de Défense Générale'. The Comité was in turn authorised to employ slaves at the service of the artillery in the batteries. Reward for such services rendered by slaves could be as great as liberty for the individual.[5] In the following year an action with the Royal Navy led to a redoubling of defensive efforts at the Isle of France. An elite corps of Noirs Courriers de la République was created and in May the Colonial Assembly ordered slave owners to send 4250 slaves to participate in the defence of the coastal batteries; a further 1900 were added to the original numbers in August 1794 (d'Unienville, 1982: 142). Magon proposed that Blacks should be mobilised for service on the batteries in case of attack. They were to be sent for exercises at the batteries every Sunday between 6 and 9 am from the first Sunday of May 1794, and were to be designated to specific duties such as 'pionniers' and 'sapeurs'.[6] In the last week of June Malartic made a personal tour of inspection of all the coastal batteries:

> *Il put constater que sous le vent les exercices se faisaient avec le plus grand zèle par les gardes nationaux et les noirs artilleurs. A l'Est cela allait moins bien et il dut rendre compte à l'Assemblée 'des batteries du vent où les gardes nationaux ne se sont pas encore rendus et où on change à chaque exercice les noirs qui y sont destinés'.* (d'Unienville, 1982: 143).

Amongst the number of these men seconded to the batteries were those slaves employed in tearing off the fibrous covers of coconuts, the material to be used for the loading of cannons. These were the 'noirs artilleurs' who trained with White gunners twice weekly. A song which presumably dates from these times was taught to me in my childhood by my Creole 'nenène'. It went as follows:

Mo papa plisse coco dans batteries canon
Mo tende piti milleton sauter
Mo ti croire l'armée anglais
qui vini qui vini qui vini qui vini. [7]

In 1791, the Mauritian members of the French National Assembly were the only colonial members to side with the Amis des Noirs and to ask for the immediate political emancipation of the free coloured populations of the colonial empire, acting on instructions received from the local colonial assembly. This attitude was quite remarkable. The West Indian deputies were astounded, and Robespierre, when he uttered the famous cry 'Périssent les colonies plutôt qu'un principe!' specifically excluded the Isle of France from this remark, in his next breath (d'Unienville, 1975: ch. 4). Could this stand of the representative from the Isle of France have been nurtured by the ties of mutual esteem and friendship forged on the ships and in the batteries of the French overseas armies?

The Heroic Exploits of Moscovite

Moscovite was a man whose humanity and selflessness shine like a beacon from the yellowing 18th century documents which record his exploits. Originally brought from Mozambique as a slave, Moscovite was owned by Philippe Paul François Vauvercy, and employed as a sailor by him. He took part in some of the most dramatic successes of French privateers over the English at the close of the 18th century, participating in the actions against both the *Trincomalee* in 1799 and the *Kent* in the following year. In the words of a British historian:

> *The capture of the Kent made a sensation at Calcutta but Bombay was more shaken by the fate of HM Sloop Trincomalee. The privateer Iphigénie, Captain Malroux, from the Isle of France, intercepted a packet called the Pearl, on 7 October 1799, at the entrance to the Persian Gulf. The Pearl was carrying treasure, which was transhipped, and Malroux meant to quit the gulf with his prize and make for his base. The Iphigénie was chased, however, by the Trincomalee and the Comet schooner. Overtaken on the 12th, the privateer engaged her pursuer, which was in fact less heavily armed. A duel with cannon ended with the privateer attempting to board the Trincomalee. That sloop lost her lieutenant, master and boatswain during the first attempt, her captain and carpenter during the second. The third attack found her with twelve survivors resisting, headed by the Purser. At that moment she blew up and sank, destroying the Iphigénie in the process, which sank four minutes later. The privateer lost about 115 men, some 30 to 35 survivors being picked up by the Pearl prize (which had beaten off the Comet). The Trincomalee went down with all hands but two.* (Northcote Parkinson, 1954: 162-3)

In 1799 Moscovite was aboard the *Iphigénie*, when that ship saw the action described above near the strait of Hormuz. When the *Iphigénie* went down, the slave used his skill as a powerful swimmer, and it was reported afterwards that Moscovite 'par son intrépidité et son courage a sauvé beaucoup de monde à la nage'. This was not to be the only time that the Mozambican distinguished himself for bravery. In the following year he was a member of Robert Surcouf's crew on board the *Confiance* and took part in the capture of the *Kent* in October 1800. It was said of Moscovite on this occasion: 'il était des premiers qui ont sauté à l'abordage'.

Moscovite's career as a man of action was not yet over. He next received honourable mention for his role on the *Petite Fanny* when that ship, which had left the Isle of France on 4 November 1805 for a voyage to Madagascar, was caught in a storm and wrecked off the north east coast of the Isle of Bonaparte. Charles François Dupont was the Captain on that occasion. He and his fellow officers, Pierre Martin, and Charles Louis Cornet of Nantes, wrote of Moscovite that he

> *a montré un courage et une intrépidité extraordinaires, en s'exposant une seconde fois à une mort presque certaine pour nous secourir tous. Après avoir donné la main pour retirer des lames les blancs qui étaient au nombre de trois, il a continué de sauver les noirs qui paraissaient, jusqu'au dernier qui lui a été enlevé des bras par la force des vagues, et qu'il n'a pu mettre à terre.*

They recommended that General Desbrulys, then commanding the island, should 'lui obtenir une récompense du gouvernement, n'en connaissant point d'autre que puisse mériter un pareil trait de bravoure'. Accordingly, on 2 October 1806, Moscovite was 'affranchi par l'Etat' according to an *arrêté* of Decaen issued at Port Napoléon. The liberated slave was rewarded with a commemorative medal in silver and a post in the public service 'aux gages qui seront arrêtés par le préfet colonial'.[8] This was a fitting tribute to an extraordinary man and Moscovite remains one of only a few slaves whose numberless acts of bravery have been recorded for posterity.

Indian and White Planters in Alliance

The rise of Indian planters as an economic elite, by the end of the 19th century, and their subsequent political aspirations, brought them increasingly into competition and conflict with the white oligarchs. But allegiances sometimes cut across boundaries of colour and community, with positive effects at times of economic crisis such as in 1929, but occasionally with devastating results, as the following saga of the Reetoo family demonstrates.

The Reetoo dynasty was founded in Mauritius by Reetoo and his wife Moteea, a married couple from Sumary near Lucknow who immigrated to the island in 1859. Their son, Kissoon was born at Constance, Flacq in the same year. A second son, Ramheet, was born in 1871. By the beginning of the 20th century, the economies of the brothers had enabled them to acquire a substantial acreage of land. By 1915 the Reetoos owned 1,350 arpents, of which 700 were planted with sugar cane, the Desfontaines sugar estate being part of their property. In 1881 Kissoon married Bugmanee, whose parents were also from Lucknow. In 1888 their son Dabeedin was born, into an already wealthy family. He used his position and the income from the plantations he had inherited for the benefit of the community through numerous social activities, including the financing of a temple and the building of schools. He is considered to have been the wealthiest Indo-Mauritian of his day (Ramsurrun, DBM: 1657-9). It was his incursion into politics, however, which marked him out as an independent thinker and which may be said to have hastened his economic ruin. In 1921 he supported Adolphe Duclos in Flacq against the Retrocessionist candidate, along with other Indo Mauritians, but at the general election of 1926 he came out in favour of the conservative candidate of the 'oligarchs', Pierre Montocchio, rather than the Union Mauricienne candidate, Rajcoomar Gujadhur. He thereby suffered a double disaster: his opposition to Gujadhur made him unpopular with the Indians; and as Montocchio whom he supported was beaten, this made him unpopular with the 'oligarchs', the euphemism for 'the Whites' party'. Within a few years he was bankrupt and dead. As this story shows, the intricacies of inter-communal relations in Mauritius are a never ending saga.

There are more edifying stories of Indian planters and Chinese shopkeepers helping out white factory owners during the 1929 financial crisis. Estate workers, for instance, were fed with goods supplied on credit by the local Chinese boutique-keeper when the estate accountant returned empty handed from the Town Office. Wealthy Indians extended financial credit to white estate owners when bills were refused by the banks at this difficult time. In this way, by adopting a common cause, more extensive bankruptcies were averted.

The colour bar which existed in the military domain until the Second World War, so that Black battalions were White officered and Indian and Coloured companies kept separate for the sake of 'uniformity', did not prevent a hearty cooperation between the different classes of soldiers, as this article has shown. Similarly, Mauritian political history is replete with examples of Indians, Coloureds and Whites rubbing shoulders in all parties, as much as they may have led separate social lives. Despite the ethnic and cultural separatism which prevailed throughout the colonial period, it is useful to remember the times when individuals seemed to act out of context, as the above vignettes demonstrate.

References

1. ANOM DFC Carton 11 Mémoire 133, Mémoire sur l'Ile de France, 14 nov 1761.
2. ANOM DFC Carton 11 Mémoire 146, Plan de deffense, utilité et bravoure des noirs à la guerre, Dumas; Carton 13 Mémoire 279, Mémoire sur la deffense et sur les fortifications de l'Isle de France, juillet 1774, Estaing.
3. MA B12/60 11 sept 1793.
4. MA B 14/44 26 juillet et 13 août , complétés par l'arrêté du 20 mars 1794.
5. MA B12/70 Projet d'arrêté par Jocet, 20 sept 1793.
6. MA B 15/14 Projet d'arrêté relatif aux noirs nécessaires à la défense de l'Isle, 11 avril 1794.
7. My father is peeling coconuts at the cannon batteries
   I heard the small mullet jumping
   I thought that the English army
   Was coming was coming was coming was coming.
8. ADR, L 33; 394; 401. A version of this story is also published in the Dictionnaire de Biographie Mauricienne: 1534-5.

Creoles & Immigrants in the 19th Century: Competition and Cooperation in Mauritius

Marina Carter & James Ng Foong Kwong

The human dimension of the socio-economic history of British Mauritius has been inadequately explored to date. The relationships between businesses, the links between wholesalers and retailers and between shopkeepers and their customers, planters and their labourers - the very cogs which kept the wheels of economy and society running smoothly - are neglected in histories of British Mauritius. This article depicts the evolution of the Mauritian society and economy after British conquest through an analysis of the complicity and competitiveness which developed between the different groups settled in and arriving at Mauritius over the course of the 19th century.

Legislation: Old and New Discriminations

During the British period, the clauses of the 'Code Noir' relative to the free coloured population remained in force, and were extended to the new immigrants arriving during this period: domestics, small traders and others. Thus the Order in Council of 8 November 1826 reconfirmed those clauses of the Lettres Patentes and Decaen's supplement to the Code Civil 'en ce qu'ils défendaient aux personnes de la population blanche de disposer de leurs biens par actes entre vifs ou par testament au profit des noirs libres ou affranchis et de profiter des dispositions entre vifs ou testamentaires que les noirs libres ou affranchis feraient en leur faveur'. However three years later, the Order in Council of 22 June 1829 abolished discriminatory legislation affecting Her Majesty's subjects of African or Indian origin. Despite this, the free coloured population continued to militate against practices which perpetuated discrimination against them, for example 'aux enterrements, partage du dépôt des cercueils avec la population servile; au cimetière, inhumation en dehors des sections reservées aux Blancs', failure to use the titles Sieur et Dame, and ostracism in the colleges. It was not until 1835 that the abolition of slavery brought about juridical equality for all sections of the population. (d'Unienville, 1979b: 38-9).

Even after this date, the coloured population had cause for grievance. In 1840 the Governor, Nicolay, forwarded a copy of his correspondence with 'respectable persons of Colour' who complained of the refusal of schoolmistresses to accept coloured girls in their boarding schools on the grounds that the parents of European girls would refuse their offspring. The Governor felt that he was powerless to act beyond the provisions of the law: 'A late Order in Council having removed from the Governor of this Colony all control over private schools, it is beyond my power to apply a remedy to this evil'.[1] Sensitivity was required concerning even the most trivial issues. When Lady Gomm took it upon herself to complete the unfinished monument to General Malartic, which stood in the Champ to Mars, by popular subscription, she did so on the condition that "this expression would proceed from all classes indifferently and that there would be no risk of gratifying any one portion of the community by the proceeding, at the expence, or to the mortification, of others.... Happily there is but one feeling of respect for the memory of their departed Royalist Governor and the coloured population are among the most active in providing funds for carrying the project into effect". [2] The British could do little more than attempt to govern as impartially as possible.

With the coming of Indian immigration, a number of new laws were passed to control this influx and to police the labour force. These laws made of labour immigrants a special category of the population, subject to pass laws and to restrictions on mobility. Ordinance 31 of 1867 representated the culmination of a series of juridical impositions specifically related to Indian indentured labourers and ex-indentureds, known as 'old immigrants' (Carter, 1995). The Indians, however, were recognised as British subjects, coming as they did from another British colony. Once they had the means to purchase a 'license' out of indenture they could acquire land and property, and many settled as small planters in Mauritius. Chinese immigrants, by contrast, were classed as aliens, and were thus affected by legislation passed in 1842 which prohibited foreigners from acquiring immoveable property (Ng, 1989: 53). But social legislation was also introduced towards the end of this migratory inflow, to provide for the offspring of unions not hitherto civilly acknowledged: Ordinance 21 of 1883 regulated the inheritance rights of natural children, and Ordinance 2 of 1890 simplified the procedures by which the division of an estate could be achieved. Marriage legislation was altered by Ordinance 28 of 1912 which provided for Hindu and Muslim priests to officiate as civil status officers. D'Unienville notes that this legislation provoked ethnic issues and religious questions which the Supreme Court could not easily answer: 'quand est-ce qu'un hindou cesse de l'etre, perdant ainsi les avantages de l'Indian Marriages Ordinance? Quand est-ce qu'un chrétien devient hindou, pouvant ainsi s'en prévaloir?' (d'Unienville, 1979b: 44-45).

Social Relationships of Creoles and Immigrants

The social consequences of a new colonial era with different priorities, at a time of profound economic transformation, when the island-as-entrepot was replaced by the plantation colony, were manifold. An initial creolization of the population occurred in the early 19th century, with the disappearance of large-scale slave trading, so that both the slave and free Coloured populations became dominated by creole-born populations, but this shift was abruptly reversed after 1834 with the huge importations of Indian indentured labour, and the service migrations which followed.

The caste identities of the 18th century began to break down along with the residential segregation of the capital along ethnic lines. Allen notes:

> *In the post-1810 era Indians also begin to disappear as a distinct subpopulation within the larger free population of colour ... the most common designation during this period is simply that of homme or femme de couleur libre. Such developments suggest that caste was becoming less important, and perhaps even irrelevant, to some aspects of free colored life as the 19th century progressed.* (Allen, 1991: 365).

However, the 'process of creating a new sense of community or common identity was a slow one' as the lack of cohesion between slaves of different castes continued to reveal into the 1830s (d'Unienville, 1975: 258).

With the abolition of slavery and the arrival of Indian - and to a lesser extent Chinese and African - labour immigrants, new forms of social contact occurred as workers of different ethnic origin found themselves accommodated together in the camps of sugar plantations. Tensions were inevitable in the early years as an almost exclusively male immigrant population - prior to 1843 - confronted a settled Creole population. Testimonies of this period indicate that one of the commonest causes of disputes between Creole and Indian labourers, was over women. Several magistrates and employers reported that Creole women had begun to cohabit with Indian men, and that this had resulted in a number of incidents involving the two groups.[3] However, one of the few women immigrants at this time, Bibee Juhooram, a Muslim who arrived in the mid 1830s, described how she was befriended by, and learnt to communicate with, local Creole women:

> *Dr. Boileau had two black Caffre girls; they were good-natured, and often did work for me which I could not do without losing my caste. When I first arrived, as they did not understand me, we could not converse at all, but latterly I learned French.*[4]

Amongst the Indian immigrants who acquired some capital during and following their indentureship, were those who determined to settle on the island and who sought marriage partners from among the class of propertied Creole women to cement their economic and social status in Mauritius. When the Indian immigrant Jonreesing died in 1884, his widow was named as Mme Izabella from Rodrigues. The property transactions of Jugputh Gopaul and his Creole wife Clemence are among many charted in the notarial records of the mid 19th century (Allen, 1983). Such alliances paved the way for the *grand morcellement* by opening up the possibilities of land acquisition to increasing numbers of ex-indentured labourers. Thomy Vythelingum, who married Marie Celina Daruty, left considerable wealth on his death in 1867: '5 plots of land with buildings on; 125 sovereigns and $157; a first class general dealer's shop; furniture, silver, jewels, a gold watch, two carts, 2 donkeys and money in a savings bank amounting to $350 in the name of his children'. The will of Vythelingum provided the following legacy for his wife and children:

Je donne et lègue à mon épouse Marie Celina Daruty laquelle demeure avec moi au quartier des Pamplemousses, la moitié en usufruit seulement de tous les biens, meubles et immeubles, que je laisserai au jour de mon décès. Pour elle en jouir sa vie durant... Et la propriété de cette même moitié à mes sept enfants légitimes Marie Adelia, Jeanne Ruisla, Jean Oscar, Marie Juliana, Marie Julia, Marie Fidelia, Michel Emanuel Vythelingum à laquelle se réunira l'usufruit au décès de leur mère.

His children were all given Christian names, but one of his daughters married a man of the same ethnic origin as her father, the Tamil Tamby Dooray, and another, Marie Juliana, married Jean Joseph Caderbaccus, a police constable of Poudre d'Or. Vythelingum's widow, Daruty, herself went on to have a relationship with one Théodore Béchard, by whom she had another child.[5] The ethnic complexity of such family groupings continued the tradition of the 'libre' families like that of Brigitte and Jean Baptiste of Chandernagore in the 18th century Isle of France.

Chinese immigrants, whose status as aliens precluded them from owning property, were quick to see the benefit of forging partnerships with Creole women (see Ng in this volume). When an Indian, Cassy, sought to take employ in his Creole wife's shop, and thereby avoid the vagrancy charges which devolved on unemployed indentured labourers, this was immediately a cause for suspicion on the part of the local police who reported:

This is a subterfuge often resorted to for the purpose of getting the immigrant population into shops, and the Creoles are paid for lending themselves to this object. In the case in question, I had no reason to believe that any legal connexion existed between the parties, and I considered the connexion assumed to be asserted only to deceive. A few Chinese have married Creole women for the express purpose of attaining shops through their wives; but this has rarely occurred amongst the Indian immigrants.[6]

In terms of the percentage of out-marriages, it was true that Indian immigrants contracted fewer legally binding relationships with Creole women. This was both a function of the earlier arrival of Indian compared to Chinese women, and the smaller number of Indian immigrants who were in a position to undertake petty commerce.

Alongside the immigration of Asian and African labour, small traders and artisans from France continued to seek their fortune amongst their compatriots settled in this British colony. Merchants, soldiers and civil servants from England further swelled the ranks of Europeans in 19th century Mauritius. Many of these individuals married into the free coloured community. Sieur Jean Boissézon, a baker by trade, arrived in Mauritius in January 1835. In April 1836 he married a Creole woman, Orthésie Parfait Coret. Employed as a baker at the house of Dame Bestel jeune, and married to a Mauritian, he nevertheless remained an alien obliged to renew his work permit regularly. In 1841 Dame Boissézon herself wrote to the Governor requesting, as 'une mère surchargée d'enfans en bas âge', that her husband's permit be renewed. In January 1842, the renewal was approved, and the family was thus reprieved for a further year. [7]

Despite the removal of juridical restrictions on marriages between different social classes, relationships might still remain unformalised if the social status of one partner did not permit its recognition. Women involved in such relationships often found themselves in uncertain economic circumstances. Adèle Breton petitioned the Governor to waive the license fee required for her to set up a shop. She explained that she had ten children, 'dont le père les aurait legitimés si sa position sociale n'y était un obstacle'. Her male partner had usually helped her with their upkeep but had recently been involved with many expenses, and so had contributed less than usual to the family income. Her request was refused. [8]

It remained relatively common for European men to take mistresses from the non-white population. In some cases such relationships were non-consensual and arose from the physical and financial power which slave owners and employers or foremen of apprentices or immigrants possessed over women. Bibi Juhooram spoke feelingly about the sexual harrassment she experienced from her employer, Boileau, in the mid 1830s:

> *he treated me very ill, gave me no pay, beat me, and said he would give me much money if I would let him have connexion*

> *with me; I told him he ought to be ashamed, that he had a wife in his bosom; that I was a Mussulmanee, and would lose my caste among my fellows, and refused, and he beat me ... I did complain to my mistress of my master wanting me to lie with him ... and she used to quarrel with my master, and threaten to break her wedding ring.* (Carter, 1994: 166)

When the Creole overseer made what Soondrum, living in the camp of Poudre d'Or estate, described as 'improper overtures' to her for a period of several months, all of which she refused, retribution was forthcoming: 'he had my boxes and property thrown out, saying the hut had been given to my husband and I had no right to be there' (Carter, 1994: 182).

However, there were also cases where love flourished across ethnic and class divides, leading to the flouting of social convention and inviting ostracism and other forms of sanction. The story of Laurestine began with the scenario of a young female ex-apprentice being sexually exploited by her employer, but ended with the disgrace of an English magistrate. An apprentice on the estate of d'Ecotay in Black River, she described having been seduced by the estate owner when she was 12 years old. By 1836, when she was around twenty years old, she was requesting help from her fellow apprentices to help her purchase her freedom so that she could leave the estate. At this stage, she came to the attention of Mr Minchin, one of the Special Magistrates sent from England to oversee the rights of apprentices. A fellow magistrate gave evidence that Minchin had described Laurestine as 'la femme la mieux formée que j'ai jamais vu'. Ostensibly to save her from the further advances of her employer, Minchin had her removed from the estate under police guard, and they began to live together. D'Ecotay complained to the Governor about Minchin's interference, and that official suspended the Magistrate from his duties. Minchin was shortly afterwards removed from the post, but it is not recorded whether his relationship with Laurestine survived the scandal.[9]

Where Creole or Indian men were implicated in attempts on the chastity of White women, the penalties were likely to be much greater than those suffered by the English Magistrate. Nimchurn, an Indian immigrant employed as a cook by a White planter, was acquitted of an attempted rape on the small daughter of his employers. The planter and two witnesses nevertheless gave a private account of the occurrence to the Protector of Immigrants and convinced him that the crime had really been attempted. As a result he recommended the following course of action to the Governor:

> *I would consider it dangerous to the peace of respectable families that such an outrageous act should go unpunished for want of those legal proofs which are seldom obtained and I would in consequence think it advisable that the man should be sent back to India at the public expense.* [10]

Indians and other non-European immigrants could not in practice be prevented from entering into relationships with consenting White women. Where this occurred, however, as in the case of the British soldier's daughter, Sally Collier, who cohabited with an Indian convict, it was generally assumed that the woman was mentally deficient (see Anderson's article in this volume).

If a male member of the White elite of Mauritius chose to flout convention and marry out of the community, his female partner and his progeny would be effectively excluded from the society of his family. Louis Furcy Arrouch, also known by his adoptive father's family name, Gerard, the son of a White Mauritian woman and a French naval captain, had a number of relationships with non-White women in 19th century Mauritius. From his liaison with one Elina Pauline, he had a child named Louise Josephine who was born in Flacq on 1 March 1824. Her birth was declared on 18 May 1840 and he recognised her as his dauughter on 7 October 1841. From another relationship with one Melanie Cartier, Furcy Gerard had a son, Georges Louis, born on 3 June 1829. He also recognised this child as his in October 1841. When he eventually married, however, it was to a woman of Muslim Indian origin. Bibijeleka Neerunjun became his wife on 17 August 1892, *in articulo mortis*. He died the following day. (DBM, 1993: 1486).

The arrival of Anglo-Indian civil servants along with the British colonial administrators provided an additional social group into which the *mulâtre* population, like Furcy's children, could marry. Henry Nicolas Beyts was reputedly born on a ship in the Indian Ocean when his mother was returning from a visit to India. He married Louise Gerard, the daughter of Furcy Arrouch, in 1841. He practised as a barrister in Mauritius before being appointed Protector of Immigrants. He became a close friend of Governor John Pope Henessy who recommended his promotion to Colonial Secretary. This was rejected by the Colonial Office, however, who described him as 'deficient in moral qualities', 'very dark' and speculated that he was 'half French and half Negro'. Nevertheless, Beyts eventually became interim Colonial Secretary and officer Administering the Government.[11]

Economic Relationships of Creoles and Immigrants

The British introduced to Mauritius, not only new population groups, but policies which brought profound economic change. With the abolition of slavery, and as the implementation of a policy of supplanting apprentice by immigrant labour began to take effect, spatial segregation took place, as Creoles migrated to the towns, or formed new settlements in coastal areas and on marginal land, and as Indian immigrant labourers clustered in camps and embryonic villages around plantations. This spatial redistribution of the working population was mirrored by the movements of Chinese, Muslim and Hindu traders and other service migrants, who installed themselves near the camps and opened shops and other services in the new settlements.

The arrival of Asian traders was not welcomed in all quarters. Anti-Chinese and anti-Indian sentiments began to be articulated in the Mauritian press from the mid 19th century against a backdrop of perceived commercial rivalry. It was fear of the undercutting of prices through the development of an Asian retail sector which led to accusations of dishonesty and traffic in stolen goods being levelled against these groups. The following article which appeared in *Le Mauricien* of 20 December 1844 is typical of the genre:

> *Le saindoux vient-il à manquer faute d'arrivages? Tout le suif du bazar est accaparé: un mélange de graisse de boeuf, de*

> *mouton, de porc et de cire est aussitôt composé et vendu au-dessous du cours. Voilà, Monsieur, comment travaillent ces hommes dont le Gouvernement semble tolérer la conduite par son silence sur leur compte (...)*
>
> *En refusant la patente à des hommes tels que les Chinois et les Indiens arrivés à Maurice et engagés comme laboureurs, le Gouvernement ne doit pas craindre de voir diminuer les rentrées provenant des patentes, parcequ'ils vont être sur le champ remplacés par des Anglais et des enfants du pays.*

Generalised attacks on one community in Mauritius, as occurred against the Chinese in mid 19th century, had several knock-on effects: firstly the community would itself close ranks against the lawbreakers within its midst, secondly, insults would be counter-traded against other ethnic groups. Insult and riposte thus became commonplace in the local press and enshrined as one of the more regrettable features of Mauritian cultural life (Ng, 1996: 118).

Within the Chinese community itself, the links between labour immigrants and traders were limited. The two groups did not operate according to the same norms and values: traders recruited new members into their group through chain migration, and controlled their activities through mutual help, discipline and internal censure. Such a network of control and assistance was unavailable to Chinese contract labour, and there is much evidence to suggest that attempts by the latter to join the former were repelled not only by the colonial authorities, but by the Chinese traders themselves. Additional differentiation within the Chinese community ran on ethnic lines, and opposed Hakkas and Cantonese. Similar divisions existed within the Indian community split into subgroups of Muslims, Hindus and Christians, which were themselves divided between merchants and labourers and by caste designation and sect appurtenance.

Nevertheless, traders, with their greater access to capital, acted as facilitators and creditors to those labour immigrants who sought to purchase land, and the felicitous combination of merchant capital and land-hungry ex-indentured workers sponsored the *morcellements* of the mid and late 19th century, when depression in the sugar market persuaded White estate owners to subdivide their large holdings. As Allen states, 'notarial acts from this era attest to the fact that the subdivision of these estates was part of a carefully planned decision in which 'old immigrants' and other Indian entrepreneurs often functioned, at least indirectly, as agents for White estate owners' (Allen, 1997: 107).

In fact, the successful integration of Indian immigrants was in no small part due to the lead taken by existing Indian merchants in advising the colonial policy-makers on the measures best adapted to the new workers. Thus Tiroumoody, a Tamil merchant and landowner settled in Mauritius, offered numerous suggestions as to the encouragement of family migration from India, leading the then Protector, Hugon, to comment 'Mr Tiroumoody takes a praiseworthy interest in the welfare of his countrymen here'.[12] The influence of Asian merchants in Mauritius ensured that the indenture system did not operate simply as a European sponsored importation of a non-White work-force. Goods from India and the staple foodstuffs of immigrants were imported by them; the ships which brought labour immigrants to Mauritius were often owned by native commercial houses in India with agents on the island. The educated government employees of Indian origin, proficient in the languages of the administration and the plantocracy (English and French) as well as their native tongues, were able to act as interpreters and petition writers for indentured immigrants. Such clerks and merchants advanced their own interests whilst serving those of the new labourers - their presence mitigated the difficulties of adaptation to a new society.

Of course, those established individuals whose contacts with new immigrants disrupted the controls put into place by the colonial state, were liable to face sanctions. As the colony made the difficult transition from slavery to freedom at the close of the 1830s, the cases of several such individuals were investigated. In June 1839, François Bernard, an Italian, who arrived in 1817 as a sailor, and had subsequently worked as a *régisseur* on several estates, was investigated. This was because he had established an enterprise on a small plot of land at Montagne Longue with numbers of ex-apprentices in his employ. Because he was known to the police as a 'receiver of goods stolen by apprentices', his case was referred to the Governor. The Carré's of the 18th century were obviously still flourishing under the new administration. In a similar case, an Indian *sirdar*, in the service of the police was sent back to India 'accused of harbouring deserters, money lending and letting convicts out of the prison'.[13]

In general, however, business relationships between different groups were conducted under the benevolent eye of the state. In 1884, Prang, an Indian immigrant, took out a loan of 300 rupees from a Creole proprietor, Robert Melotte, 'pour l'aider dans ses besoins et affaires'. The interest was set at 12% per year. In the same year Eugène Patron and Auguste Desenne sold land to Hindu labourers and A. Corentin sold a small plot of land to the Muslim Goolam Hassen. Occasionally the trend was reversed, as Indians also leased property or sold land to Creoles.[14]

It was not always labourers who were on the receiving end of such deals. As British subjects, Creole ex-apprentices and Indian immigrants were in a position to purchase land and property which was denied to the non-naturalised Chinese, designated aliens. Following the acquisition of land by ex-apprentices during the *petit morcellement*, and by Indians during the *grand morcellement* from 1860, these groups joined the White estate owners in leasing land and shops to Chinese traders. The following table provides an indication of the extent of such transactions and their significance for the development of the Chinese retail trade in Mauritius:

Leases made to Chinese Immigrants, 1870-1910

Landholders	**No of Leases**	**% of Total Leases**
Indians	94	50.26
General Population	53	28.34
Sugar Estates	10	5.36
Transfers between Chinese	30	16.04

Source: Ng, 1984: 56, from a sample of notarial acts

Those Chinese who had already settled in Mauritius, marrying local women and becoming naturalised, were able to purchase land and shops from other ethnic groups. Significantly, when they sold on, or leased their property, they did so principally to other Chinese settlers. This was particularly true for the Hakka immigrants who started arriving as from 1860, whose sense of clan belonging was strong, as can be illustrated by the undertakings of members of the Lee clan. In this way, the community came rapidly to acquire a dominant interest in the small retail sector across the country:

Sales of Businesses between Chinese and other Ethnic Groups, 1870-1910

Vendors	No of Acts of Sales	% of Total Sales
Chinese to other Chinese	124	34.83
General Population to Chinese	77	21.65
Chinese to General Population	38	10.67
Indians to Chinese	64	17.97
Chinese to Indians	46	12.92
Institutions to Chinese	7	1.96

Source: Ng, 1984: 58, from a sample of notarial acts

The notarial records provide further details of individual transactions which illustrate the processes through which land passed from Whites to ex-apprentices to the Chinese. For instance, in 1843 Baptiste Minerve and his wife purchased a small plot of land from François Maissin. In 1875 it was sold to Lee Ah Van, a Chinese trader in Black River. The land in question bordered the main road, which was significant, because shopkeepers were required to situate their boutiques in view of the police station and close to principal roads.[15] It may be speculated that Ah Van was moving in to this district to service the growing community of ex-apprentices who had settled in Black River. Other Chinese leased land within sugar estates, intending to serve as shopkeepers to the Indian labourers who worked on the property. In 1874 members of the Bourgault Ducoudray family of Flacq accordingly leased to Lee Chong and Choolong

> *une portion de terre de trente pieds carrés de superficie à prendre sur la propriété l'Union ... la dite portion de terrain bornée, la face par le chemin qui conduit de la maison*

principale à l'usine de la propriété; et des trois autres côtés par la dite propriété l'Union.[16]

In this case, the lease was for a period of two years. Other estates leased land for periods as long as 9 years, but attached conditions such as requiring the lease-holder to build the shop for the estate, detailing the size and design of the building. Mrs Ducoudray specified the construction of 'une boutique de vingt pieds de long sur quinze pieds de large et douze pieds de haut, au moins, en poteaux et planches et couverte en tôle ou fer-blanc'.

In some cases Chinese retailers were taking over from previous shopkeepers. In 1867 it was recorded that Emile Beugue leased to 'Chinois Jeenchoa no 1042 marchand de Terre Rouge ..... une boutique en bois, couverte en bardeaux située à Rivière des Calebasses, Pamplemousses'. When Chung Teang acquired the lease from the Central Sugar Estates Company, he was taking over a shop which had already been built by Sieur Sabapady. In 1884, Bhunjun no 241,487 leased his shop, with attached kitchen to a Chinese trader, Ah Yan. Shops thus came into the hands of the Chinese not only through marriage with Creole women (as Ng shows in this volume) but through general commercial transactions, and often because previous incumbents had not made a success of the enterprise. In 1852 Anne Marie Alexandrine, a shopkeeper of Grand River, finding that she could not make a proft from her small grocery and spirits business decided to sell the business to a Chinese immigrant, Achiai. In this manner, the Chinese gradually acquired a predominance in this sector.[17]

In the second half of the 19th century, as more Indian labour immigrants acquired land through the *grand morcellement* they increasingly figure in leases acquired by Chinese immigrants. The conditions attached to the leases made by Indians were generally more flexible than those imposed by the owners of sugar estates, because the Indians depended more directly on the leases as a source of revenue. Sub-letting and the ceding of leases between further parties were practised by the Chinese, with the sanction of Indian landholders, so as to enable them to expand their commercial activities and at the same time to open up the retail sector to new arrivals from China. For example, in 1894 Seeyave was able to cede the remainder of his lease to Lee Hee Sing, 'passager de Hong Kong'. Some proprietors were even willing to reduce their rent when business conditions were unfavourable for their Chinese lessees. The Muslim landholder, Ahmed, agreed in 1905 that 'en raison de la fermeture de la boutique élevée sur la propriété Ste. Marie et de la réduction des affaires des susdites boutiques, le loyer de Rs 325 est réduit à Rs 225', at the request of Li Sing & Co. Such terms suggest the mutual dependence of the Chinese lessees and the landholders in these transactions.[18]

Land transactions between ethnic groups were not always to the advantage of the purchaser. Rungen's petition claimed that he had been cheated on the lease of his market garden by a Creole woman:

> *I was a mirchant to selling vegetable thing and for the named Madam Frances; last 26th October 1872 this grount about three quarter of arpens for lease she gave with me for five years. Shee maid a deemand papper with me and so I was worked in it about two month .... I lost much money for cutting grount and building a house and putting some vegetable things in it and then shee neaver tell with me, Shee sold the garden with one man Ramasamy shopkeeper at Bellerose and so my Lord I got more fore years and five month from that grounts. They will push me out of the garden how can I go O my Lord and then I went with Mr Gonuss at the Polis I told with him and there he gave a letter for the madam and I carryed that letter with madam shee not accept that letter and put down... O my Lord, the man of Ramasamy he took all the vegetable and then he told to me do not go in-side the garden and so I beg by your Honor Company Magestrat to give me a garden about my time that she made a papper for me till fore years and five months O my Lord.* [19]

Dwareeka and Gooroodyal had a similar tale of hardship. Having, they believed, purchased a plot of land from a Creole, when they wished to sell it they found that the notary who had drawn up the bill of sale declared that they were not at liberty to dispose of the plot as they wished *your two Petitioners having on the 16th September 1872 purchased three acres of ground at Vacoua from one Volsy Ambrose for the sum of $150 which bill of sale was drawn by notary V. Barry. who charged the Petitioner $25 for drawing of the said bill of sale... Sir, nowe your two Petitioners in desire to sel the same plot of ground befor the said notary to a party desire to purchas; the said notory totelly refuses to sel our part. Your Petitioners therefore begs that your honour will look in to our poor circumstances, and know from the said notary the reson for what Defeculty he nowe finds on our desire, if the said plot of Ground was not fit to be sold or purchast, than did he sel to us. We therfor beg for your honour justice.* [20]

Despite such difficulties, commercial transactions between ethnic groups were generally to the mutual benefit of both. This is well demonstrated by the extensive system of loans which enabled new immigrants of various denominations to start up in business, helped by longer established communities. The following table provides an indication of the extent of such inter-communal systems of credit:

Loans and credit granted, 1870-1910	*Number*
By Chinese to General Population	112
By General Population to Chinese	87
Between Chinese	32
By Indians to Chinese	23
By Chinese to Indians	22
By Chinese to Institutions	4

Source: Ng, 1984: 103, from a sample of notarial acts

The above table demonstrates the special relationship which existed between the Chinese and the general population (comprised of Creoles and Whites), but also demonstrates the business confidence between the Indian and Chinese communities. This extended to links between wholesalers and retailers: Chinese traders in the rural districts depended for the supply of their goods on Muslim wholesalers in Port Louis who dominated the commerce in grain and cloth and on white merchants who controlled the remaining sectors of import/export activities.

This inter-dependence was also crucial to the successful take-over of certain sectors of the economy by one ethnic group from another. When the Chinese moved into the distillery business, it was Whites who provided the land and machinery for the new producers. Similarly, when the Chinese decided to manufacture cigarettes in Mauritius, they depended on Indian tobacco cultivators for their supplies. [21]

It was in the towns, and especially Port Louis, however, that the Chinese shopkeepers serviced their widest clientele. The Fukinese were the earliest Chinese traders to settle in Mauritius and they established shops on the northern edge of the White quarter, or Ville Blanche. The commodities on sale at Hahime's shop at no 83 Royal Road, for example, included fine wines, eau de cologne, and Chinese porcelain, suggesting that members of the White community, and of the Creole middle class were consumers of such luxury merchandise, alongside the essentials of life which the humbler classes could also purchase from such establishments. [22]

The evidence of mutual dependence in commercial undertakings did not mean that fierce competition and antagonisms were not present in the business history of Mauritius. Towards the end of the 19th century, the spirit of inter-ethnic business co-operation which had contributed so much to the success of the Chinese traders in establishing themselves in the retail trade, was called into question by a section of the White and Coloured population. In 1894, white members of the Legislative Council gave vent to this expression by announcing:

> *La vérité est que la colonie est envahie par les Asiatiques et que la population créole est graduellement écartée de toutes les branches du commerce et de l'industrie ... nos finances sont aujourd'hui à la merci des (Chinois). Déjà le commerce des grains, qui alimente notre population, est entre les mains des arabes, ... le jour n'est pas éloigné où les Indiens seront maîtres du pouvoir politique.* (Debates of Council, vol II, 1894: 1750, 1794)

The stage was set for a debate which sought to demonstrate that the Chinese had taken over the retail trade to the detriment of other population groups. The British colonial administration was fortunately circumspect in resolving the crisis. Responding to a proposal that Chinese traders should be subject to a special tax, the Colonial Secretary reminded the gathering that the said community in Mauritius

> *comprises of a great number of British subjects and naturalised citizens of this colony ... It is the primary duty of all governments to give equal protection to all classes of the community ... we cannot surely think that the Government will agree to the ruin of one class in order to protect another.*(1864-5)

The ethnic specialization which had occurred in certain sectors of the Mauritian economy was simply the result of the cumulative advantages of family, kin or clan-based business relationships. It could not have taken place at all without the implicit and explicit support of other groups through leases, land and property sales and credit facilities.

Economic relationships between groups eventually led to close personal ties which acted as a defence against outbreaks of xenophobia. As an example J. Joly, whose wife rented land to Indian smallholders at Grande Rivière, took a close interest in their welfare. In 1868 he complained to the Protector that in spite of having tickets with photos as required by law, the men had been refused the delivery of passes. They were later arrested in their houses as vagabonds by the police and Joly went to the local Stipendiary Magistrate who then set them free. Others, forced to sign engagements rather than go to prison, subsequently asked Joly to get their contracts annulled. Similarly, when the Tamil merchant Soopramanien Nadar, of Rose Hill, wrote to the Protector of Immigrants in 1908, about Mrs Boodhoo, it was from the simple desire to help her better her circumstances. As he informed the Protector, the woman was a

> *poor widowed mother named Noorun Budhoo, immigrant of 1875, No. 378,152. Her unfortunate husband has departed his life some months past and left her with three little children unprovided for and that she endured great hardship. I took pity of the woman. I gave her room from charity, from time to time I gave her a little help on account of her children. I therefore most respectfully pray you to grant her a monthly allowance to take care of the said children. Should an inquiry be made to assure the veracity of the statement it will be proved to your*

entire satisfaction, very often the unfortunate woman and her 3 little children stay dinnerless, praying for a speedy reply. [23]

There is no doubt that such humanitarian acts were part and parcel of the process of economic integration, wherein ties regulated initially by mutual self-interest developed into personal relationships of mutual respect.

It was in joint business undertakings, such as those described in this article, which saw Whites, Indians, Chinese and Creoles employed across a whole range of artisanal and industrial pursuits, that the development of a typically Mauritian business ethos gathered pace, and the spirit of co-operation for mutual benefit which has been a characteristic of the island's history, took root. Economic interdependence therefore acted as an inhibitor of communal confrontation which was always latent in a society undergoing as many changes as were experienced in 19th century Mauritius. This conjunction of socio-economic factors still plays the same role of safeguarding political stability in modern Mauritius.

References

1. MA SD 18/16 Nicolay to Russell 13 Feb 1840
2. MA SD 27 Gomm to Gladstone 27 July 1846 (141)
3. PP 1837-8 lii (180) Queries and Replies made to Indian Labourers by Magistrates, 1835-7.
4. PP 1841 (45) Examination of Bibee Juhooram Aug 1838.
5. MA PA 14 Marie Célina Daruty to RC 28 June 1873; NA 109/2 MAINGARD jan - juin 1867, 26 jan 1867. Testament Thomy Vythelingum; NA 117/23 PLANEL 1884 2 juin 1884 Inventaire après décès de M J Vythelingum; NA 117/23 PLANEL 1884 26 juin 1884, Inventaire après décès de Jonreesing.
6. MA RA 1019 Report of Commissary of Police, 22 June 1849.
7. MA RA 675 14 Jan. 1841 Petition of Dame Boisségon.
8. Idem, Petition of Adèle Breton, 14 Jan 1841.
9. PRO CO 167/192 Nicolay to Glenelg, 17 Oct 1836. The case forms the subject of an entire volume of Colonial Office proceedings: see CO. 167/193.

10. MGI PL 32 Protector of Immigrants to Colonial Secretary 2 May 1848.

11. A Moheeputh, L'Express, 13 June 1992.

12. MA RA 1129 Hugon Report 31 May 1851.

13. MA RA 583 Police to Colonial Secretary, 3 Oct 1839; RA 584 Civil Commissary to Colonial Secretary 11 June 1839

14. MA NA 117/23 PLANEL 1884 3, 9 avril, 1 mai and 10 juin 1884

15. MA NA 116/7, Acte de vente, 2 sept 1875; Ly Tio Fane, 1983: 88.

16. MA NA 107/105 Bail, 21 août 1874.

17. MA RA 1183 Petition of Anne Marie Alexandrine 23 March 1852; NA 109/2 MAINGARD 7 jan 67; NA 116/66 Bail 27 nov 1883; NA 117/23 PLANEL 1884 4 avril, 15 mai 1884.

18. MA NA 124/52 Transport de Bail 28 août 1894; NA 124/94 Prolongation de bail 24 mars 1905.

19. MA PA 14 Petition of Rungen, 18 May 1873; Immigration Department Note, 22.5.73.

20. MA PA 14 Petition of Dwareeka and Goordyal.

21. MA NA 121/4 Acte de la Distillerie Pékin, 10 août 1880; NA 109/10 Acte de Vente, 28 mai et 2 juin 1890.

22. Le Cernéen, 25 April 1840.

23. MGI PL 79 J Joly to Protector of Immigrants, 28 July 1868; PL 25 Nadar to Protector of Immigrants, 10 Feb 1908.

Convict Socio-Economic Autonomy in 19th Century Mauritius[1]

Clare Anderson

'The negresses will go to the convicts and the convicts will come to them ... I try all I can to stop them - it is impossible'.

MA Z2A65. Letter from W. Clover, Chief Overseer of Convicts, to J. Finniss, Chief of Police, August 12th 1831.

Between 1815 and 1837, some 1500 Indian convicts were transported to Mauritius. They came from the Presidencies of Bengal and Bombay and the island of Ceylon: most of them never returned to India. They were a disparate group, made up of Muslims, high-caste Hindus, shudra peasants, *dalits* (untouchables) and tribal *adivasis.* What they had in common was that they had all been sentenced to transportation to the island for either life or a term of years, with their criminal offences ranging from theft and *dacoity* (gang robbery) to plunder and murder. The number of convicts received on the island was extremely limited in comparison to the 453,000 indentured Indian immigrants who arrived after the abolition of slavery in 1834 (Carter, 1995:7). However, it was significant enough to make a demographic impact on a population which, according to the first census in 1826, totalled 9,000 Whites, 14,000 Indians, Chinese and Creoles and 63,000 slaves.[2]

After their arrival, the convicts were put to labour on public works projects, which included clearing land, quarrying and building and repairing roads and bridges, including the first suspension bridge at Grande Rivière and the original Pont Colville. With a rapid expansion of sugar cultivation on the island, making improved communications vital, it is clear that the convicts were a valuable labour force. Indeed, after the abolition of transportation to Mauritius, numerous complaints arose about the poor condition of the roads. It has also been suggested that the experience of the utility of convict labour influenced the later decision to import indentured Indians to work on the plantations (Nicholas, 1988:32). If it did not influence it, it certainly facilitated it. Thus a Commission of Enquiry (1875) reported that the previous existence of 'convict forced labour' made the Mauritian Indian indentured labourer 'not the entire stranger he was in the West Indies and Demerara'[3]

Convicts in Mauritius were cut off from their former social networks through their transportation. It was believed that this, together with regular work and strong discipline, would effect their moral improvement (Maxwell-Stewart, 1997:142-62). Concerns were also expressed that convicts should not interact with other ethnic groups on the island. During the early years of the convict system, relations with slaves and apprentices were prohibited. In 1823, all 'illicit intercourse' between the convicts and others was strictly forbidden. Clear instructions were issued:

> *The convicts are not to wander about the Country, or to go to the Houses of the Inhabitants, nor are Soldiers, People of Color, or Slaves, to be permitted to frequent the Convict Camp ... every precaution should be taken to prevent illicit intercourse with the Indians or other Inhabitants of Port Louis.*[4]

As the immigration of Indian indentured labourers accelerated in the 1830s and 1840s, convict relations with these people became the focus of concern. The Chief of Police, John Finniss, wrote of the increasing number of Indian labourers 'whose morals are not likely to be improved by their intercourse with the convicts, (the natural consequence of their speaking the same language)'.[5] This combination - removing, working, segregating and disciplining convict bodies - was perceived as key to the success of transportation.

The convict system did not operate on the strict discipline and segregation which colonial rhetoric claimed, however. In practice, although the convicts were put to hard labour, their surveillance often left much to be desired. The wide distribution of working parties made it difficult to control them. In 1820, it was said that there was 'not a place belonging to the department where a convict might be put in with anything like security'.[6] In 1832, 500 convicts were said to be 'dispersed in open camps, without guards'.[7] By 1835, the situation had not improved.

A Convict Camp in the South-East of the Island

The Chief of Police complained that the convicts were still 'scattered about the districts ... without any place of confinement at night'.[8] Convicts quickly became integrated with the wider population, particularly slaves, ex-slaves, the Creole population and the Indian community. Given that the system's utility required the convicts to be working throughout the island, often on a temporary basis, there were few practical counter-measures that could be taken. At the same time, the difficulties of effectively institutionalising control became apparent.

Convict cohabitation and family life

Perhaps the most enduring manner in which the convicts negotiated their place within Mauritian society was through family relationships. On their arrival, it was directed that the convicts should not mix with the existing population, including Mauritian women. However, although many convicts left families in India,[9] many more established intimate relations after their transportation. It is significant that there were never any allusions to 'unnatural crimes' (sodomy) amongst the convicts, as there were in the more isolated penal settlements elsewhere in Southeast Asia. Inevitably, numbers of convicts also had children.

Hutted in open camps all over the island, the convicts found it easy to slip away to their concubines at night. At the same time, women were able to gain access into the camps. Cohabitation became an integral part of convict life. Indeed, by 1842, it was said that the convicts 'reside where they please'.[10] The convicts' ability to find concubines reveals several interesting phenomena. It exemplifies the relative freedom with which they eluded the surveillance of their camps. It shows them as willing and able to interact with both non-convict Indian women and women of alien ethnicities and cultures. Social interaction and cohabitation, particularly with non-Indian women, also implies that at least some of the convicts acquired the lingua franca of the island, creole. In a colonial situation where males far outnumbered females, evidently at least some of the convicts possessed material resources adequate to attract partners and support family dependants. Moreover, such relationships were tolerated and even supported by certain authority figures, as a means of encouraging social stability.

There are many examples of convict cohabitation during this period, whether with free women, Indian women, slaves or apprentices. In 1828, the slave Charlotte was arrested when she was found with her 'husband', a convict. She was later released from police custody when her master, Sr André, declared that he had given her permission to go and visit the man.[11] In 1831, the convict Symdaker was arrested together with the slave woman Euphrasie, whom he claimed was his wife.[12] A maroon slave woman, Dorinde, was also said to be living with a convict.[13] The convict Abdullah stated that his wife, Angélique, was a government apprentice who lived in Port Louis.[14]

This is not to say such relationships were friction-free. In 1829, the woman Marie Elisabeth came to complain to the police that her husband, the convict Soucramamode, had taken all her clothes and refused to give them back. She said that she had left him because he frequently beat her, a charge which Soucramamode denied. The police eventually persuaded

Marie Elisabeth to go back to her husband on the condition that he should behave better in the future.[15] In 1831 Marie Elisabeth again went to the police. She stated that her 'real' (or perhaps 'new') name was Bertie Pierrot, that she was aged about twenty-three, and had been a slave until she was emancipated by Soucramamode two years' previously. However, he had since died, leaving her destitute, so she wished to be placed on government rations.[16]It is a strange paradox that at the same time as she was disassociating her name from slavery in the most literal of senses (becoming Bertie Pierrot), he was still a convict, though relatively wealthy. At the same time, allegations that he had 'mistreated' her suggest that he may have viewed her as personal property of a similar kind to a slave.

Other convicts used financial incentives when seeking concubines. In 1829, two slaves claimed that the convict John Marian Decosta had given them money to try and persuade them to live with him. Jenny and Félicité, Widow Rouillard's maid and seamstress, were given ten *piastres* each. They told their mistress of the proposition when they realised that the money was stolen.[17] In 1832, another convict, Kindrie, complained to the police that the slave Louison, with whom he had cohabited for six months, had left him, stealing his cloth and thirty-seven *piastres*.[18] Presuming that his savings were hidden, possibly buried, she was clearly well aware of his concealed wealth.

Sally Collier, the daughter of a soldier in the 29th Regiment who had left Mauritius several years previously, also cohabited with a convict named Meerwangee. Her choice of a convict partner was explained away on the grounds that she was 'of very weak intellect'.[19] However, she had a daughter named Sarah and a young son, for whom she presumably needed to find means of support.[20] Whether he was the children's father or not, Meerwangee may have been a sound financial bet. Although the records do not reveal whether Sally Collier was White or Eurasian, it is possible that her father had seen service in Bengal and, even if her mother was not Indian, she may have spoken Hindustani. At the same time, there was no barrier, at this time, within plebeian British society, to White women having sexual relations with African or Asian men (Myer, 1990: ch. 7). Therefore Sally Collier was breaking the social taboos of a sugar colony with its structure of White rulers and masters and a non-White workforce, but she was not violating any working class social taboo of her times. Her relationship with a convict clearly transgressed the boundaries of colonial expectations, however, and was only rendered comprehensible through doubts about her mental stability.

The competition for the limited number of women in the colony sometimes precipitated convict domestic violence. In typically orientalist fashion, these were commonly characterised by colonial officials as crimes on account of 'sexual jealousy': the actions of the 'hot-blooded native'. Domestic violence, rather than being simply a 'crime of passion', resulted from the imbalanced sex ratios in the colony. Of the 15,000 Indian immigrants who arrived in Mauritius between 1834 and 1839, for example, between 1-2% were female. By 1845, this figure had risen slightly, to just 6%. Not until the 1850s did women account for 40-50% of the total number of indentured labourers received (Carter, 1995: pp. 89 & 91-2; Lal,, 1984: 48). Convict violence against women may also have been linked to the defence of *izzat* (honour). The possibility that a woman did not show total *patrivrata* (devotion) to her husband could lead to *sharam* (shame) before the whole community. In this context, a woman who even spoke to another man besides her husband may have been liable to a beating (Mandelbaum, 1988). Mauritian female slaves, apprentices and free Blacks may not have felt such a restraint in their personal relationships. A culture-clash could, therefore, occur when they became intimate with Indians.

In 1827, Rumuth Kan (alias Cassal) was found guilty of arson on the night of April 10th at the establishment of Sr Faduilhe in Savanne. Twelve slaves' huts were burnt down. Cassal had a former concubine, a slave called Melanie, who belonged to the establishment. She had left him to live with another slave, Jean Baptiste, over a year before. Cassal tried several times to try and persuade Melanie to return to him, sometimes using violence. On one occasion he had knifed her in the neck, beaten her with a stick and attempted to strangle her. He had also threatened to burn down her hut about a month before the fire. Although Melanie did not see Cassal on the night of the fire, she believed that he had started it. Cassal admitted that he had fought over Melanie, but denied setting fire to her hut. He claimed that he was 'very attached' to her because they had a child together. However, the evidence against him was very strong. The threats he had made against Melanie during the preceding months were witnessed by several people and he was arrested on the night of the fire while hiding in a nearby hut.[21]

This epitomises the type of case in which colonial officials were quick to ascribe violent assaults to 'sexual jealousy'. However, there was often no evidence for what were little more than cultural stereotypes. In 1843, for example, the convict Limbah Poonjah was sentenced to two years' forced labour for the attempted murder by stabbing of another convict, Nathoo Dunjee.[22] The circumstances were never fully clarified. On that night, Nathoo had been asleep in his hut with his concubine Fanny when Limbah came in and attacked him with a knife, for no apparent reason. The court immediately assumed that the attack resulted from Fanny's infidelity with Limbah. However, this was never proved, with Nathoo stating that he had never doubted his wife's fidelity and that he had never argued with Limbah. Limbah testified that he had been drunk on that night and could not remember what had happened.[23] Alcohol seems a more likely explanation than testosterone here.

In another case of 1845, the Chief of Police wrote of 'a most horrible murder'. A young child named Bidacy had been found brutally strangled. Suspicion immediately fell upon the Bombay convict Kittoo Ramjee.[24] He had once cohabited with the mother of the child, Sidonie, a Creole seamstress living in the Camp Malabar. Bidacy was Sidonie's child by an Indian named Baziratti with whom she had cohabited before she met Ramjee. She then lived with Ramjee for nine or ten months. After this, she left him to go and live with another Indian named Ramdiane, who worked at the Port Louis bazaar. Finding that Sidonie had a new lover, Ramjee threatened both of them. It was said that he killed the child as a result of circumstances which 'excited his jealousy'.[25] Ramjee remained in prison to complete this sentence, even after the last of the convicts were liberated in 1853.[26]

As for the small minority of women transported to Mauritius, it was inevitable that they would have sexual relations with other convicts.

Mussomaut Bhurovee, for example, who arrived in the colony in 1816 had two children by 1818, Lockey and Duhive. It was stated that she had lived with 'some of' the convicts.[27] By 1824, she had given birth to a third child. In 1829, the sole female convict from Ceylon also had two children.[28] The Bombay convict Ragoo had a child, 'a little boy', by 1852.[29] Colonial officials made clear judgements about the women's character, viewing them as promiscuous and of poor moral virtue. Evidence of the very existence of female sexuality invariably led to a less than favourable characterisation. Upon the expiration of their sentences in 1848, for example, two convict women were said to be 'bad characters'.[30] There is no evidence of any previous misconduct on their part.

In contrast, the male convicts' ability to establish families often won them support from the authorities. The convict Gearnoo Dannoo was pardoned in 1849 after requesting permission to find paid employment as he was the father of five children.[31] Mullala Solimon also had his petition of liberation approved as it was said that he had a wife and five young children whom he 'seems anxious to do his best to provide for'.[32] Hurry Bappoo, a life convict from Bombay, petitioned the Protector of Immigrants in 1858. He stated that he had a five year old daughter, Luckchemee, whom he wished to send back to his family in Bombay with his wife 'where she would be better off'. He could not, however, afford the £2-10 cost of the passage. He said that he had cohabited with the Indian woman Succool who had arrived on the island in 1843 as an indentured labourer and now wished to return to India. Although the Indian authorities had refused to grant his request to return to India, the Protector of Immigrants in Mauritius agreed to pay the cost of his wife's passage.[33] It is clear that the authorities viewed the convicts' ability to support families as a stabilising social force.

Convict religion

The social autonomy which convicts established in their personal lives, despite their 'unfree' status, extended into other areas. In 1823, convict overseers were instructed not to interfere with the 'religious habits or prejudices' of the convicts, in what was clearly an effort to promote social stability. At the same time, the lack of surveillance over the convicts gave them the opportunity to participate in religious activities together with the general population, which was against colonial directives. The convicts came from two main 'religious' categories. The majority were described as Hindus (55%) and a substantial minority as Muslims (32%). Another small minority (14%) were of adivasi origin.[34] Given that the convicts came from wide tracts of North, Northeast and Western India, there would also have been significant regional differences between the groups. At the same time, amongst Hindus, caste status may have influenced religious practices.

Muslim convicts had strong links with the general Muslim population. In 1832, Gassy Sobdar, a religious leader, complained about their burial. He stated that Islamic practices regarding the burial of the dead had been violated, with 'a convict of another religion ... buried in a place specially reserved for the burial of Muslims'. According to Gassy Sobdar, a number of Muslim convicts had also been buried without a religious service. He went on:

> *[I] take the liberty of stating that the religion and those that believe in it pose no threat to the interests of the government, and to suggest that an order be given to the guardian of the cemetery that no body which is not accompanied by a Muslim priest be buried there, and to bury the bodies of those convicts who are not Muslims outside the place designated for those who are.*[35]

Although there is no surviving evidence of an official enquiry into his complaints, it was directed that the convicts be consulted.

Convicts also attended the annual Yamsé festival. Although the origins of the festival in Mauritius can be located in the eighteenth-century Muslim community in Port Louis, it quickly became an inter-religious event, with other communities taking part (Carter, 1995: 261-2). The convicts also became involved, with the opportunity to participate in festivities presenting the chance to escape from the everyday drudgery of working life. In 1838, a police circular stated that 'serious disorders' had taken place after fighting broke out between the convicts and other

Indians.[36] As a result, convict processions in the districts were banned and celebrations were confined to the convict camps.[37] This directive was largely ignored: in 1841 there were more disturbances between convicts and other Indians during which a convict was injured. In 1843, fighting again took place; apparently as a result of a convict's sexual involvement with a free Indian's wife.[38]

Convicts and the acquisition of private property

Another aspect of convict social autonomy was the acquisition of private property. In 1817, George Smith, the Chief Judge of Mauritius, wrote: 'beyond the possession of life [the convicts] have no other property'.[39] Two years later, they were formally prohibited from owning any personal effects.[40] Despite this, personal possessions in practice became an accepted feature of everyday convict life. The limitations of surveillance allowed convicts to participate in transactions, both legal and illegal, with each other and the wider population.

Property was accumulated for personal consumption or as a medium of exchange. Poultry, goats and clothing supplemented government rations. Clothing and jewellery may even have become a marker of status, with petty luxuries gained for personal use. The sale of such goods and others, such as cloth or silverware, could also be very lucrative. Overseers and other officials eventually came to accept the *de facto* existence of convict petty property. In 1847 it was directed that convicts could hire themselves out to free individuals after they had finished work, formalising the unofficial mechanisms through which the economic integration of the convicts in Mauritian society had already been assured.[41] Such property was stabilising and perhaps also encouraged convicts to become partly self-supporting. This had obvious fiscal benefits for the colonial state.

Some convicts supplemented their rations or made money from breeding and selling poultry or goats at the Port Louis bazaar.[42] In 1831, overseer Boyle Finniss acknowledged buying five chickens from the convict Samdoby at a cost of $1.35. Pirhally and Purshadoo, too, sold poultry and goats.[43] Samdoby did laundry for the Chief of Police to earn extra cash. Other convicts earned money as carpenters or builders after normal working

Grand River, where the convicts had a camp

hours. Mooktaram Goindah, for example, stated that he earned extra money by working as a mason in the evenings and on Sundays.[44]

Other convicts became involved in illegal activities: theft, robbery and the trafficking of stolen goods. In 1831, three government apprentices were found guilty of burglary. They confessed to selling the stolen goods to a convict named Basarate Can, who was subsequently accused of receiving them. His story was that he had been working on the road at Grand River when a man came and offered to sell him a shawl and three necklaces. On enquiring whether the goods were stolen, the vendor had assured him that they were not. Basarate Can took the goods on credit, promising to repay four *piastres* within four days, whilst planning to resell the goods for at least twenty rupees. As it could not be proved that Basarate Can had known that the goods were stolen he was acquitted.[45]

The large difference between the price he paid for the goods, and the price he anticipated receiving for their resale, suggests he was well aware that a receiver could strike a hard bargain with a thief. The transaction also reveals that goods were being exchanged on credit terms, which speaks for the relative economic sophistication of these men. One suspects a reproduction in Mauritius of Indian petty credit practices. Indeed, in 1839, a bond for $50 was found in a convict's hut in Port Louis. The convict stated that he had obtained it under the promise of paying six rupees per month interest to a free Indian *sirdar* who was attached to the police.[46]

In a similar case, Saquias and Soomir were accused of receiving some jewellery after Mme Durup was burgled. Durup's servant told her mistress that her friend Virginie, who cohabited with a convict at Plaine Magnan, had a gold comb of the same type as one which had been stolen. The police questioned Virginie at the convict camp. She claimed the comb was given to her by her partner, the convict Saquias. He claimed to have purchased the comb in Port Louis for six *piastres*. A search was made of the convict camp and some other jewellery was found in Soomir's hut; Soomir provided the same explanation. Both men pointed out an Indian named Bocary as the man who had sold them the goods.[47]

Several convicts also acted in concert with other individuals in committing crimes against property. In 1838, Seckhossen was convicted of stealing clothing and personal effects belonging to the watchman of a plantation. The watchman, Charlin, had allowed Seckhossen and his non-convict accomplice, Ramchand, to stay the night in his hut. After he fell asleep, they robbed him.[48] In 1840 Doulale and the apprentice Mélanie were convicted of stealing a goat belonging to Sr Graves. They then sold it to another woman for the sum of seven *piastres*.[49]

There were also allegations that the convicts were involved in melting down stolen goods made out of precious metals. In 1845 it was discovered that indentured Indian immigrants were taking silverware to be melted down by a convict silversmith in Moka. The convict camp was obviously relatively open. The Chief of Police, wrote:

> *I have on several occasions brought to the notice of government the facility given to the theft of plate, watches &c. by the promptness with which it is known they are melted down in some of the Convict Camps ... Under these circumstances I*

would beg leave to suggest that the convicts should not be allowed to have utensils of this nature in their possession, and that orders should be given to the overseers to assist the police in their researches.[50]

As a result of police enquiries, an order prohibiting the convicts from melting down coins or working in gold or silver was made.[51]

In a similar case, the convict Lada and an Indian named Faquira were found guilty of forgery.[52] For some time, neighbours had suspected the two men. They called the police, who discovered them working in Faquira's yard, with a large cooking pot containing some rupees over charcoal embers. Several small bags of money were also found wrapped in the Lada's *dhoti*. When Faquira's house was searched, a trunk containing a quantity of iron and welded metal was also seized. Faquira denied the charges, asserting that he had hired his yard to some convicts in the belief that they made jewellery. He claimed to know nothing about the forging of coins. Lada also stated that he had been making some rings when he was arrested. However, there was a substantial amount of evidence against them and the two men were both sentenced to twenty years' forced labour.[53] Forging coins was clearly a good opportunity for the convicts to increase their personal wealth. In another case of forgery of a different kind, eight Indian labourers were arrested in the district of Savanne in possession of forged old immigrant tickets. They claimed that they had bought them from a *sirdar* on their old estate. When questioned, he stated that he had bought the tickets from the convict Manuel Dominique Debras for $5 each. Manuel did not deny the charges, having made a quick profit of $40.[54]

Convicts' relative degree of freedom to interact with the general population laid the ground for periodic conflicts. Wide involvement in economic exchange inevitably led to disputes about money. In September 1821, for example, the convict Same was accused of robbing the Creole woman Marie Louise Mayon, who lived in Flacq. Marie Louise claimed that she had been assaulted by a group of convicts until she lost consciousness. She came round several hours later, realising that she had been robbed of a substantial amount of jewellery and the sum of almost

$300. Four religious engravings were also missing, together with a trunk containing all her clothes. Louise Pierre Morice, Marie Louise's servant, was present at the time of the robbery. She recognised Same as one of the assailants because he had frequently been to the house to sell rice. Also, as Same confirmed, she had often been sent to the convict camp to buy rice from him. On the day of the robbery, according to Louise, Same told her that if Marie Louise did not pay him three *piastres* she owed for rice, he would come and beat her.

On the morning after the robbery Marie Louise went to the convict camp to make a complaint against Same. She admitted that she had not yet paid for some rice bought from Same, claiming that she did not have enough money to do so. Same denied the charges against him, although he said that he had often given Marie Louise rice and poultry for which she never paid.[55] This looks like the motive for the assault and robbery. Lacking other means of redress for breach of contract, Same appears to have decided to demonstrate that he was not a man to be cheated.

Convicts themselves were also the victims of disputes over money. In 1830, a fire broke out at the Black River camp; the convicts' huts were completely destroyed. Their overseer, Simon Thatcher, suspected that the fire had been started by maroon slaves and the camp was moved to a new site in Bamboo.[56] In 1831, it was again the target of an arson attack. Thatcher wrote:

> *There is a family of coloured people living close by, that have been in the habit of selling liquor to the convicts - on Saturday there was a dispute between them and the Convicts respecting a marquee. On the night of the fire, between seven and eight o'clock, the overseer had not left the sentry two minutes after giving him particular instruction to be on the alert (afraid in consequence of the dispute that something might occur) when he called out fire, at the same time he, the sentry, saw a man run from the rear of the huts followed by a dog.*[57]

The arson attack was, Thatcher continued, the result of a dispute over money which the convicts owed the Creoles for alcohol. Socio-economic interaction inevitably sometimes led to conflict.

The convicts transported to Mauritius were not a segregated social group. Despite their 'unfree' prisoner status they integrated into Mauritian society, through intermarriage, religion and their economic activities. Given the lack of control over the convicts, it is unsurprising that they were also able to retain a degree of social autonomy. Indeed, the establishment of family relations and continuity in religious practices were an integral part of convict life; generally tolerated by the authorities as a means of fostering social stability. Despite initial objections, convicts were also able to acquire personal property. Lapses in surveillance allowed convicts to carry out both legal and illegal economic transactions with the general population. Indeed, the existence of convict property ultimately came to be seen as a boon to the system. It opened up the prospect of allowing property as an incentive to good behaviour and encouraging a degree of (economic) self-dependency. If convicts became self-supporting, it removed a degree of fiscal pressure from the colonial state. The separation of the convicts as a discreet ethnic community was thus of no benefit to the convicts and, still less, to the colonial authorities themselves.

References

1. I would like to express my gratitude to Dr Crispin Bates and Dr Ian Duffield (Department of History, University of Edinburgh) for their suggestions on earlier drafts of this piece. I am also grateful to staff at the India Office Library (IOL) and Public Record Office (PRO) in London; the staff at the Mauritius Archives (MA) in Coromondel; and, to Dr Marina Carter who aided me enormously during an extended research trip to Mauritius in 1995/6. The research was financed by the British Academy and Carnegie Trust for the Universities of Scotland, to whom I would also like to express my thanks.

2. PRO CO172/42 Baron d'Unienville, Tableaux de Statistiques, tableau no. 6.
3. PP 1875 XXIV Mauritius (Treatment of Immigrants): Report of the Royal Commissioners appointed to inquire into the Treatment of Immigrants in Mauritius, p. 27.
4. MA Z2A70 Letter from W. Staveley, Head of Convict Department, to J. Finniss, 4 September 1832.

5. MA Z2A92 Letter from J. Finniss to G.F. Dick, Colonial Secretary, 25October 1835
6. MA RA135 Letter from F. Rossi, Head of Convict Department, to G.A. Barry, 13 May 1820.
7. MA RA525. Letter from W. Staveley to G.F. Dick, 31st January 1832.
8. MA Z2A92. Letter from J. Finniss to G.F. Dick, 25th October 1835.
9. PRO CO167.124. The Commissioners of Eastern Enquiry suggested that 286 of the 1018 convicts hitherto received had left families in India, including 270 wives and 446 children. Appendix 23: Return of the number of Indian Convicts at Mauritius, 30 October 1824.
10. MA RA708 Letter from J.A. Lloyd, Surveyor General, to G.A. Barry, Colonial Secretary, 23 February 1842.
11. MA RA365 Police report, 12-13 December 1828.
12. MA RA457 Police report, 21-22 November 1831.
13. MA Z2A72 Letter from J. Finniss to G.F. Dick, 26 August 1833.
14. MA JB281 Trial of Abdullah. Police report, 2 October 1835.
15. MA RA365 Police report, 11-12 December 1828.
16. MA RA451 Letter from J. Finniss to J. Smith, Acting Chief Secretary to Government, 2 March 1831.
17. MA JB221 Trial of John Marian. Interrogation of Jenny & Félicité, Court of First Instance, 7 September 1829. John Marian Decosta was of 'Portuguese' descent, probably originating from the Goan region of India.
18. MA RA473 Police report 10-11th January 1832.
19. MA Z2A106 Letter from J. Finniss to G.F. Dick, 6th July 1838.
20. MA Z2A122 Letter from G.F. Dick to J. Finniss, 4 May 1837 and Z2A132. Letter from J. Finniss to G.A. Barry, 25 July 1840.
21. MA JB180 Trial of Rumuth alias Cassal. Police report, 14-15 April 1827; evidence of the Court of First Instance, 7 & 23 August, 27 June & 29 September 1827;and, verdict of the Court of Assizes, 29 September 1827.
22. MA JA77 Verdict of the Court of Assizes, 29 June 1843.
23. MA JB377 Trial of Limbah Poonjah. Police report, 14-16 March 1843 and evidence of the Court of First Instance, 17-18 March 1843.

24. MA JB347 Trial of Kittoo Ramjee. Letter to J. Finniss, 12 September 1845.

25. MA JB347 Trial of Kittoo Ramjee. Statement of the Procureur Général, Court of Assizes, 17 March 1846.

26. MA RA1198 Governor's Minute on the Liberation of the Indian Convicts, 15 Feb. 1853.

27. MA RA180 Letter from F. Rossi to G.F. Dick, 8 June 1821.

28. MA RA262 Letter from F. Rossi to G.F. Dick, 26 June 1824 and MA RA411 Letter from H. Bates, Head of Kandyan Prisoners, to G.F. Dick, 7th May 1829.

39. MA RA1164 Report of a Medical Committee 23 November 1852.

30. MA RA973 Letter from J.A. Lloyd to G.F. Dick, 5 April 1848. Such characterisations were also common amongst women in the Australian colonies.

31. MA RA1043 Petition of Gearnoo Dannoo, 22 October 1849.

32. MA RA1118 Petition of Mullala Solimon, 29 January 1851.

33. MA PA 6 Petition of Hurry Bappoo, 15th January 1858 and report of the Protector of Immigrants, 14th January 1858. Marina Carter, 1996: 6,13 also cites this.

34. Compiled from convict ship indents available in the IOL (percentage figures rounded up to the nearest whole number).

35. MA Z2A70 Letter from Gassy Sobdar to J. Finniss, 3 September 1832.

36. MA HA105 Police circular no. 264, 19 February 1839.

37. MA HA105 Letter from J. Finniss to Plaines Wilhems' police, 2 March 1839.

38. MA JB332 Trial of Massoobene Ramjee, Sackoo Puddhoo & Aribapou. Statement of the Procureur Général, 16 September 1843 and medical report of Dr R. Allan, Acting Police Surgeon, 12 February 1843 and MA JA77. Verdict of the Court of Assizes, 9 October 1843.

39. PRO CO415/15 Letter from G. Smith, Chief Judge, to G.A. Barry, 20 July 1817.

40. MA RA132 Letter from F. Rossi to G.A. Barry, 23 August 1819.

41. PRO CO167/287 Report of a Committee, 20 July 1847.

42. MA JB239 Trial of Charles & Narcisse. Police report, 20 July 1831.

43. MA JB183 Evidence of the Court of First Instance, 4 January 1827 and MA JB239 Trial of Charles & Narcisse. Police report, 20 July 1831.

44. MA JB211 Trial of Mooktaram Goindah. Evidence and verdict of the Court of First Instance, 12-13 March & 3 April 1830.

45. MA JB277 Trial of Basarate Can. Evidence of the Court of First Instance, 14 Oct. 1830 and verdict of the Court of Assizes, 23rd June 1831.

46. IOL P.402.46 Letter from J. Finniss to J. Burrows, Captain of Police Bombay, 3 October 1839. Bombay Judicial Proceedings, 27th May 1840.

47. MA JB334 Trial of Bocary, Saquias & Sommir. Evidence of the Court of Assizes, 13 March 1834. Unfortunately, there is no record of the verdict in this case.

48. MA JA63. Police Correctionelle, 20 April 1838.

49. MA JA69. Police Correctionelle, 21 August 1840.

50. MA RA824 Letter from J. Finniss to G.F. Dick, 5 May 1845.

51. MA RA824 Report of J.A. Lloyd, 5 May 1845.

52. MA JA52 Verdict of the Court of Assizes, 4 April 1834.

53. MA JB268 Trial of Lada & Faquira. Police report, 27 August 1833 and evidence of the Court of First Instance, 2, 7, 11, 13 & 15 November 1833.

54. MA RA824 Letter from J. Finniss to G.F. Dick, 12 May 1845. Old immigrants were required to obtain a ticket which acted as proof of having completed their period of service (Carter, 1995: 200-1).

55. MA JB138/JA88 Trial of Same. Evidence of the Court of First Instance, 16 June, 17 July & 4 October 1820 & 8 September 1821; police report, 11 May 1820; and, verdict of the Court of Assizes, 8 September 1821.

56. MA RA429 Letter from S. Thatcher to W. Staveley, 7 December 1830.

57. MA RA429. Letter from S. Thatcher to W. Staveley, 11 October 1831.

The Construction of Communities: Indian Immigrants in Mauritius

Marina Carter and Vishwanaden Govinden

The subcontinent of India incorporates within its borders a multiplicity of languages, cultures and religions. Representatives of many of these ethnic groups embarked on the migrant ships which brought indentured labourers to Mauritius. In the process of reconstituting an ethnic identity in their country of adoption, Indians from different regional and linguistic groups intermarried and were subsumed into new 'communities' generally predicated along religious or caste lines. Thus, Muslims arriving from the different Indian states, intermarried to constitute an Indian Muslim group, unified by a common labouring origin and distinguished from the Muslim mercantile class by the appellation 'Calcuttiya'. Yet the name of this new 'community' reflected only its largest component, those Muslims who migrated from northern India via Calcutta. The Muslim labourers who came from regions as diverse as the Punjab, Bombay and Tamil Nadu were subsumed into the larger group, and their linguistic and cultural specificities disappeared. As the Muslim case demonstrates, religious identity overrode regional and linguistic characteristics to become the primordial distinguishing feature of Indians. Immigrants from the subcontinent identified themselves in Mauritius as Christian, Hindu and Muslim. Within the Hindu community, caste created further sub-groups. The purpose of this article is to reappraise the characteristics of the 'communities' constructed through the settlement of Indian immigrants in Mauritius. The data outlined below highlight the disappearance of numerous linguistic minorities such as Bengali and Malayalam speakers in Mauritius and demonstrate that each of the new 'communities' formed, is in essence a blend of Indianness in all its dimensions.

Under the indenture system which was operational in Mauritius between 1834 and 1910, around half a million Indians arrived in the colony. Approximately a third of that number returned to India on the expiry of their terms of contract; the remainder settled in Mauritius. The pace and characteristics of the immigration were controlled by economic conditions, employer preferences and legislative enactments. Thus, sex ratios were enforced by law, from 1855, requiring that at least one third as many women as men be dispatched on every vessel sending migrants to Mauritius, whilst employer demand regulated the size of the annual contingent of recruits shipped. Family migration was encouraged by pecuniary incentives which rewarded men for bringing their wives. As a result, between 60% and 80% of all women arrivals were married or migrated in family groups. The vast majority of married couples had contracted caste endogamous unions in India. Only 26 of 1039 arriving married couples sampled by Carter (1995: 94) were caste exogamous. These included several cases of Brahman males with wives from the *vaish* group, or of *vaish* males with *shudra* spouses, and several Hindu/Muslim partnerships. Recruitment was channelled through the principal Indian ports of Calcutta, Madras and Bombay. Calcutta supplied the largest number of immigrants, and Bombay the smallest. Within these regions certain districts provided a disproportionately greater number of recruits. From north India, Bihar and UP sent most migrants, in which states Shahabad, Arrah, Ghazipur, Gya, Gorakhpur and Azamgarh were heavy contributors to the indentured population. Tamils and Telegus arrived primarily from coastal districts such as Vishakhapatnam and Madras, and the adjacent districts Chittoor, Thanjavur, Chengalpattu and Tiruchchirappalli, whilst the majority of Marathis were from Ratnagiri, Thane, Malvan, Savantvadi and Satara (Carter, 1995: 108). The French territory of Pondicherry, with its trading links with French colonists, supplied many early recruits. At the same time, migrants from as far afield as Kabul in Afghanistan, Mozambique in Africa, and Canton in China also arrived as indentured labourers on ships from India, and were included in that category in the registers of the colony.

Despite the heterogeneity of the indentured population, and its dispersal after arrival to the various sugar estates around the island, regional and linguistic clusters did re-form in Mauritius, assisted by a pattern of immigration which incorporated the recruitment of large kin and family groups from particular villages and their settlement around plantations. This process was assisted by the heavy involvement of Indian *sirdars* in the recruitment and shipping of their compatriots. On one ship which arrived in 1846, all 59 immigrants on board were Assamese. Regularly, groups of 10 or 20 migrants would collectively embark. Whilst such groups might be split into smaller bands on arrival, depending on the numbers of labourers required by individual planters, several persons from one village could still be allotted to the same plantation, with the possibility of later regroupment within Mauritius of the larger number. The majority of Indians who migrated to Mauritius were Hindus, Muslims formed around 25% of the total number, and Christians a small minority.

The Settlement of Hindu Indians in Mauritius

An important means of self-definition for Hindus was through the caste system, which influenced choice of marriage partner, and other life-cycle events. The caste status of overseas migrants was recorded on emigration certificates, and was more accurately compiled for Calcutta migrants than for recruits travelling via Madras or Bombay. Linguistic status and region of origin were also significant identifiers. Some of these forms of self-classification have survived into modern Mauritius, but more interesting for the purposes of this article is to study those minority linguistic and regional groups within the Hindu population which have disappeared and presumably been absorbed into other sub-groups.

Marriages contracted in Mauritius between Indian immigrants were recorded in the registers which had been established upon each individual's arrival in the colony. The existence of this data provides a unique glimpse into the process of partner selection. From a sample of 165 such marriages contracted between male and female immigrants, 17, or approximately 10% were contracted between individuals who had arrived on the same ship, reinforcing the popular perception of the importance of *jahaji bhai* networks. Sex disparity amongst first generation immigrants meant that a bride-price was often paid by prospective grooms to the future parents-in-law, and that widows experienced little difficulty in remarrying in Mauritius. The vast majority of the immigrants who married in Mauritius contracted intra-regional marriages: Mahrattas, Telegus, Tamils and North Indians generally acquired a partner from within a common linguistic, if not a common caste group (Table 1). Only 8 of 165 marriages sampled were inter-regional, ie 7 between South and North Indians and the single remaining case being an individual from the Bombay Presidency with a Bihari.[1] When James Bapoo married Murden Pechayee, in 1874, the marriage was both inter-regional and inter-religious. Murden was a Tamil Hindu and Bapoo, a Maharashtrian who had embraced Protestantism.

Table 1

Marriages of First Generation Immigrants in Mauritius - Region in Spouse Selection

Spouse Data	**No of Cases**
Intra-Regional Marriages	
Bengali	4
Telegu	14
Tamil	28
North Indian	41
Maharashtrian	5
Inter-Regional Marriages	
North/South	6
North/Western	2
Same District Marriages	
Ghazipur	4
Thanjavur	6
Tiruchchirappalli	1
Vishakhapatnam	12
Ganjam	2
South Arcot	1
Gaya	1
Arrah	2
Ratnagiri	2
Purulia	1
Unknown	33
Total Cases	165

Source: Carter, 1995: 248.

The influence of caste in selection of a marriage partner was weakened in Mauritius because caste endogamous unions were more difficult to arrange, but immigrants adapted by looking for partners from among the caste communities to which they were most closely related. Endogamy was in most cases replaced by the most acceptable alternative: hypergamy, which in the Indian context enabled high caste males to take wives from lower castes. From a sample of 165 marriages between first generation immigrants there are numerous cases of Chamar females marrying up: to Brahman, Ahir, and Gowala males. Similarly women from the Vaish categories, for example Koiri were also considered acceptable wives for Brahman males. However, those individuals who belonged to castes for which there were numerous potential partners, were in many cases able to contract intra-caste marriages. Thus, Chamars, Nonias, Koiris, Kurmis, and Burryeks were able to find suitable marriage partners from within their caste (Table 2). Significantly, these are among

Table 2

Marriages of First Generation Immigrants in Mauritius - Caste in Spouse Selection

Spouse Data	**No of Cases**
Inter-caste marriages	103
Same caste marriages:	
Chamar	6
Nonia	3
Maratha	4
Malabar	21
Yatha	1
Gentoo	9
Kapu	1
Koiri	3
Kurmi	2
Kumbhar	1
Salee	2
Burryek	3
Paria	2
Rajput	1
Odda	1
Telegu	1
Kahar	1

Source: Carter, 1995: 259.

the caste groupings which remain important in Mauritius today, reflecting the continuity of the larger socio-religious units to which many migrants belonged.

As other contributions to this volume have indicated, considerations of property and status also influenced choice of marriage partner among immigrants, and Hindus were no exception to this. A celebrated case of an inter-regional marriage of two propertied individuals was that of Songor Itty, from Madras, and Doya Kishto, of Midnapore. Songor, who had arrived in 1843, was a *sirdar* on the Clemencia estate. Doya Kishto was the widow of another immigrant from Calcutta, and Songor became her second husband. They were both owners of plots of land near the estate when they married in April 1859. Among the witnesses at their wedding was the owner of the estate - Pierre Amourdon Arlanda. Their names are remembered today, because they are credited with the building of a Tamil temple on their land (Sooriamoorthy, p. 130-4). Evidently, a common Hinduism was more important than a regional affiliation for Songor and his wife. Similarly, Dabeedin Reetoo, despite being of North Indian origin, donated a portion of land at St Julien d'Hotman for the erection of a *kovil* or Tamil temple (DBM: 1658).

Doya Kishto was from Midnapore, in Bengal, and one of many Bengali speaking migrants who came to Mauritius. An indication of the importance of their contribution to the Indian community is the fact that of a sample of approximately 5,000 immigrants' districts of origin, between 1834 and 1874 Bankura in Bengal supplied 338, and was the fifth largest district sending recruits (Carter, 1995: 108). Further, of a sample of 165 immigrants who married in Mauritius, 8 were Bengalis, all of whom married within their linguistic group (Table 1). It seems clear then that a sizeable Bengali-speaking community was in place in mid 19th century Mauritius. Statistical research has yet to ascertain how many Bengalis were of Hindu origin, since the main sending districts from Bengal are those with high concentrations of Muslims. Traces of Hindu Bengali immigration can be found, however. Luffur, from Bankura, was of the *dom* caste; he came to Mauritius on the *Lord Hungerford* in 1859. Yet today, aside from a few family names which recall a Bengali Hindu origin such as Roy, they have all but disappeared. No doubt, most Bengali Hindus have married into the Bhojpuri-speaking group.

Another disappeared sub-group of North Indian immigrants are the sizeable tribal populations who arrived in Mauritius in both the early and late waves of indentured arrivals. The proportion of tribals who migrated to Mauritius in the first decade of indenture seems to have been significant. A British Indian official estimated that of 7,000 Indians who went to Mauritius in 1837 and 1838, approximately one-third were tribals.

Indian Migrants Awaiting Embarkation

The same official calculated from annual statistics compiled at Calcutta, that the total number of tribals despatched to Mauritius between 1842 and 1870, was more than 50,000 individuals (Carter, 1995: 104-5). Ship registration data in Mauritius confirms the importance of tribal immigration. Almost half the immigrants on the *Apolline* which arrived in April 1844 were tribals and they amounted to 20% of all those aboard the *Marion* in 1846. Tribals or *adivasis* were not classed as Hindus, but considered as animists, and were thus outside the caste system. Instead they were designated by the generic term *dangar,* or hill coolie or by specific tribal names such as *mundars, oraons, gonds* and *kols.* Heavy mortality ratios among tribals who were depleted by endemic cholera in Calcutta, led to a reduction of the activities of recruiters in the tribal or hill districts, but in the late 19th and early 20th century, numerous *kols* and other tribals reappeared on the migrant ships arriving in Mauritius. As a category, however, they seem to have disappeared, perhaps their descendants have been subsumed into the *shudra* sub-grouping of Hindus.

A similar story of linguistic disappearance has been the fate of South Indian minorities, such as Malayalam and Kannadi speakers. In the early 20th century a number of immigrants of the Nair caste from Cochin arrived in Mauritius. This coastal port in the state of Kerala is Malayalam speaking, and some of the group settled on the island. Kedeyaparambil Kistnan who arrived as a 25 year old, died at Grand Port in 1905. Immigrants from Mysore and Bangalore in the state of Karnataka would probably have been Kannada speaking. These linguistic minorities no longer survive in Mauritius and probably married into the larger Tamil and Telegu speaking South Indian communities. In this way, the present day Bhojpuri, Tamil, Telegu and Marathi Hindu communities are themselves composed of numberless subgroups who have been absorbed into larger linguistic and regional communities.

The Settlement of Christian Indians in Mauritius

The presence of a Christian Indian community in Mauritius is well known and predates the large-scale arrival of labourers from the subcontinent in the 19th century. Nagapen and Moutou have charted the immigration of Catholic Tamils from the early years of French occupation. Nagapen reports that free Tamil Christians had their own cemetery at Salines from 1772 and played an active part in Church activities (Nagapen, 1984:11). The ranks of this community were swelled by the arrivals of Christian Indians from South India with other indentured immigrants. Amongst the earliest indentured Indians was a couple named Elizabeth and Chourimootoo, who arrived in the 1830s and worked in a family as *ayah* and cook respectively. They returned to Pondicherry on the expiry of their indentures in 1842 (Carter, 1994: 40).

The majority of Christian immigrants arriving during the 19th Century were from South India. Tanjore and Trichinopoly were common regions of origin of Tamil Christians, six arrived from the former on the *Minden* and eight from the latter region on the *Scindian* in 1858. South Indian Christians had a distinctive nomenclature. Names such as Chavry and Savrimoutou are a reference to St Francis Xavier. The first names of Tamil Christians were often variants of Hindu names; the surnames are often directly linked to Catholic Saints. Thus, in 1861 the arrival of Davasagayen Chouremootoo, a 22 year old Christian from Trichinopoly is recorded. Names such as Anthony appear frequently in the case of men; however Tamil first names such as Arokium and Yangapen were very often retained. Whilst very often only two or three Christians are recensed on an individual ship, in some cases, they travelled in large groups. On the *Eskadale* in 1859, 42 Christians arrived from the Tamil districts and on the *New Great Britain* in the same year, 72 Christians immigrated; they came principally from Kistnapuram, Madura and the Vepery district of Madras. There were also Christians from Portuguese enclaves such as Goa. Manuel d'Silva arrived as a 32 year old on the *Mount Stewart Elphinstone* in 1861. A number of Christians from Cochin arrived on the steam ship *Wardha* in 1902. Three were listed as Roman Catholics, two of whom were named Joseph. Another immigrant, also called Joseph and from Cochin was surprisingly listed not as a Christian but as a 'Raman Nair'. Rama Menon from Calicut, also in Kerala, would also have been a member of this linguistic group. The language of these Keralans was Malayalam. Kannada speaking Christians also arrived from Bangalore and Mysore.

A smaller number of Christians arrived from North and Western India. The 32 year old Kistodoss from Purulia was listed as a Christian in the *Regina*'s ship register despite his Hindu name. On the same ship, which arrived in 1858, was the 25 year old Samuel Baker and the 16 year old Eliza, both from Calcutta, probably Protestants. Antony, a 27 year old Christian from Chaprah, emigrated to Mauritius in 1859. These Christians would have been Bengali and probably bhojpuri-speaking, respectively. The likelihood is that they married into the Creole speaking Indian Christian community and the linguistic specificity of the small Bengali speaking Christian community was no doubt soon lost.

Some Christian immigrants also arrived via Bombay. Rosine Fernandez, a 40 year old widow from Bombay, embarked for Mauritius but was rejected on arrival. A group of Christians who migrated to the island from Bombay in 1864, were listed as hailing originally from Mozambique. Amongst them was a married couple, Yassin and Fatima Francis whose names suggest that they were converts from Islam. Exactly when Bombay immigrants Rumma and Peter Luckman became Catholics is unclear. Rumma arrived in Mauritius in 1859 as a 7 year old with her parents Govindseth and Chimma. She was from the village of Mahad in Tanna, and the family were Hindus. Rumma died young, aged 25, when she was declared to be a Catholic. Her husband, a shopkeeper named Sewoobudden, also died early, aged 31. They had two children, Marie Cecile, born in Port Louis in 1870 and her younger brother Joseph. The children were the owners of several houses at Vallée des Prètres, which had belonged to their father. Some time after their parents' decease, they were confided to the care of their grandfather, Govindseth, on condition that half the income from the house rents was to be paid into a savings bank for the children. He claimed that the houses were destroyed in a cyclone and failed to do this. In 1880 he came to the Office to obtain consent to marry the 10 year old Marie Cecile. This was not given. When Govindseth died, the children were placed with an uncle, evidently a Christian, as he was called Peter Luckman, and also an immigrant from Bombay. A year later, however, when the girl was 11, Luckman himself succeeded in marrying her to a man named Sirjappa.

When Marie Cecile was 14, she and her 11 year old brother came once again under the scrutiny of the Immigration Office when Peter Luckman complained that Marie Cecile was about to be married off to a man named Sunputh, whom he declared to be 'an invalid and quite unfit to be married'. The girl and her brother were now living with a Hindu woman named Rajoo, mother of the boy. Marie Cecile declared to the Protector however, that she had no intention of marrying the son, who was paralysed and claimed that as both her husband and Luckman had "beat and ill used her", she preferred to live with Rajoo. It is likely that the property owned by the children was one reason for Marie Cecile's abundance of suitors. The Immigration officials were greatly impressed by her maturity and the responsibilities she had undertaken in managing the houses and the rental income on her own. Her story indicates the continuing inter-relationships between Christian converts from Hinduism and their Hindu fellow-immigrants. [2]

It seems likely that Christians arriving from India as indentured labourers are under-represented, in statistical terms, because of the inaccuracy of the caste data, under which religious denominations were recorded. For example in the ship register of the Mermaid which arrived in September 1858, the caste of all those on board is listed as Malabar, a designation usually taken to indicate a Hindu religious affiliation. However, a considerable number of those on the ship have names which suggest a Catholic appurtenance, such as Chavrimoutou and Arekioum. And, in fact, the register of married couples on the ship lists 14 such couples who are designated this time, not as Malabar but as Christian.[3]

Since the majority of Christians arrived from Tamil speaking areas, and shared a language in common with their Hindu fellow immigrants there was a considerable overlap between the two groups. Intermarriages between Christian and Hindu Tamils were not uncommon. For example, Chauremootoo, a Christian Tamil from Salem who arrived as an 8 year old on the *Myrtle,* married the Tamil Hindu Rajamah at Rivière du Rempart in 1876. Of 165 marriages sampled, two were between South Indian Hindu females and Christian Tamil males (Table 1).

Many Christians undoubtedly married into the Creole Catholic community already settled in Mauritius. Nicholas Pike devoted a chapter of his 19th century travel account to "The Marriage Ceremony of the Madras Malabar Indians" in which he described a wedding he attended in Moka Street, Port Louis, between a Tamil Catholic, Thomas, and his Hindu bride, Pomona:

> *When she was properly seated, the groom took his place beside her on the sofa. The priest then lighted a small fire and poured oil over it, which he dipped from a basin with a maize leaf. He then sprinkled rice over the shoulders of bride and groom, and held towards them a copper dish filled with rice, bananas, and coconuts. They both had their hands filled with the mixture .. and everyone, down to the smallest child, placed both hands in it ... The bridegroom then placed a yellow silk cord round the bride's neck .. The priest again came forward and tied the ends of their robes together to prevent the demons from touching them ...*(Pike, 1873).

Christians from linguistic groups such as those from Bengali or Malayalam speaking regions were no doubt obliged to marry into other religious or linguistic groups. In some cases Christian Indians married converts. Thus in 1876 George Davis, probably a Protestant, judging from his name, who had immigrated as a 10 year old from Masulipatam, married Emilia in Riviere du Rempart. She had arrived as a Muslim girl, named Assabee, but had been converted to Christianity as a result of her orphaned state and subsequent upbringing at the Protestant-run Powder Mills Orphan Asylum in Mauritius. By the third quarter of the 19th century, when Indian orphans were consigned to the Barkly

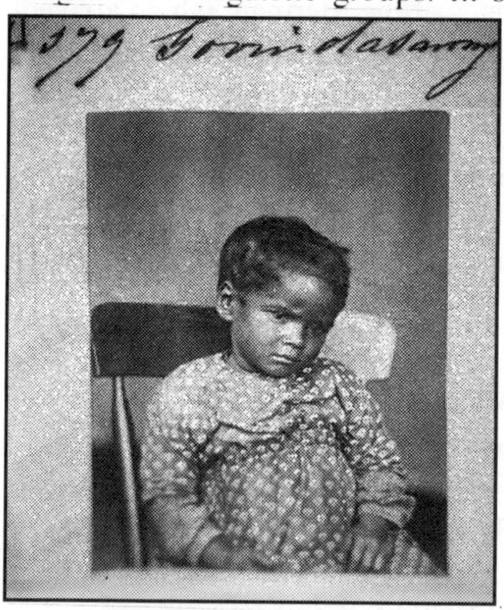

An Indian Orphan

Asylum, such establishments were still run by the Protestant Church, but it was the belief of the colonial administration that

> *In a Government Establishment, there should be allowed no derisive or condemnatory remarks as to the religion professed by any of the inmates. If these are not checked bad feeling is likely to result. No interference should be allowed with the religion of an orphan child which may be assumed to be the religion the child's parents belonged to or professed.* [4]

In practice of course, orphaned children continued to be influenced to adopt either the Catholic or Protestant faith. When the Poor Law Commissioner visited the Asylum in 1877, he discovered that Catholic staff employed by the Protestant director of the establishment had been actively proselytising their charges to abandon Protestantism and embrace the Catholic faith. At that date there were 45 orphans resident at the Asylum of whom 24 were Creoles of Catholic parents, six were Indians baptised as Catholics before coming to the orphanage, and five were Indians baptised as Protestants since their arrival. In addition, ten Indian children not yet baptised were being instructed both by the Reverend Buswell and by Father Daribère, a jesuit.[5]

Many such children expressed a natural wish for integration into the Christian Creole community when they were of age. In 1880 Essoo petitioned the Governor to be able to change his name, so that he could contract marriage with a fellow Christian. Arrived in Mauritius in August 1858 as a child with his parents, he had been orphaned in December of that year. He was then confided into the care of John Villecollet and his wife. He wrote

> *Que suivant les exemples qu'il a eu sous les yeux, il a voulu se faire baptiser dans l'année 1864, et qu'il est resté sincèrement depuis 16 ans à la foi chrétienne.*
>
> *Que par la nature de ses relations pendant 22 ans de séjour dans le pays, il a adopté entièrement les moeurs et coutumes des familles créoles, et qu'il désire aujourd'hui contracter mariage avec une jeune fille créole. Que la famille de la jeune fille et celle-ci consentent à cette union projetée sous la condition que votre pétitionnaire demandera à votre autorité*

supérieure, Excellence, la sanction nécessaire de votre part, pour que votre pétitionnaire puisse changer son nom de Essoo en celui de Joseph sous lequel il a été baptisé.

His request could not be complied with, minuted the Colonial Secretary, because 'the law empowering the Governor in Executive Council to allow family names to be changed only extends to ex-slaves and persons whose births have been registered in Mauritius'. The Procureur General confirmed 'There is no law which authorises an Indian upon his baptism as a Christian to change his name'.[6]

Catholic Tamils were assisted by the religious network which was already in place for this community. Reverend C Neyrolles petitioned the Protector for free passages for such families who wished to return to India with their Mauritius-born children in 1907. His letter mentioned Sinnapen and his wife Ceciliamma, with their child Dorasamy, alias William, and Rajapen, his wife Arokiamma, and their children Sandapa and Rayapen of Belle Vue Morel, and finally Joseph Mootien and his wife Madaleimma. [7]

Marie Louisa Kameereddy became 'une religieuse indienne de la Congrégation de Notre Dame des Sept Douleurs', and resided, in late 19th century Mauritius, at the order's house at no 4 Rue Coton. She was the acknowledged natural daughter of one Kameereddy. Her mother or step-mother was Papee, alias Paupamah no 237,850. Paupamah had arrived as a 17 year old in 1859 on the *Duke of Malakoff.* She was a Gentoo (Telegu) from Ganjam, as was the father, judging by his name. How Marie Louisa became a Catholic nun is unclear. She and her brother, baptised Louis Noel, might have come under the wing of the Catholic Church, after their father's death.[8]

Slaves, like orphans, tended to convert, because they found themselves alone, without religious ties, in a Christian environment. Zamor Bongout, an Indian slave who became a successful restaurateur in the early 19th century, converted to Christianity at the age of 57 and donated a plot of land to the Church at La Prairie. He constructed the first chapel of Sainte-Croix on the site, which was inaugurated in 1848. On the death of Père Laval in 1864, it was to Sainte-Croix that his remains were taken. Thus Zamor's plot of land has become a place of pilgrimage (Nagapen,

1984:12). In other cases the children of immigrants, educated at Christian schools and mixing with their fellow pupils of this faith, were inclined to marry into the Creole community, as Pike noted in 1873. He attributed this to the habit of Indians of

> *bringing up their children after Creole fashion, by giving a smattering of education in French and English: and when such children attain to their age, they are inclined, against the will and consent of their parents, to marry a Creole young man or Creole young woman ... These boys and girls desire Creole connections simply because they associate with that class of people from their infant days, and whose language they had adopted.... Hence convivial mingling and inter-marriages are in daily practice here.*

However Pike was of the opinion that 'Inter-marriages have tended to produce bad results', without enlarging on his reasons. (Pike, 1873: 482). This was a prejudice shared by many of his contemporaries towards the relationships which were being forged between newly arriving ethnic groups in Mauritius.

The Settlement of Muslim Indians in Mauritius

As with Christians, Muslims arrived during the indenture period from diverse regions of India, with different cultural and linguistic traditions. The majority were from the Bhojpuri speaking regions of North India, but significant numbers of Bengali Muslims also came to Mauritius, and smaller numbers from South and Western India, so that Tamil and Marathi speaking Muslims must also have arrived on these shores. Thus on the *Mariner* in 1861 arrived Ebraham, a 28 year old Muslim from Trichinopoly, South India and in 1865 Mariam Luximon, a 20 year old Muslim from Bombay, disembarked from the *Caroline*. Punjabi speaking Muslims also arrived from that state: Syed Meera, and Cootboodeen in 1865, and Essay Khan in 1864, for example. Ebrambee, a 28 year old Muslim from Bangalore in the Kannada speaking state of Karnataka came to Mauritius in 1861. Muslims from Lucknow, Kurruckabad and other districts of northern India would probably have been Urdu speakers.

An African Muslim who arrived from Bombay in 1864

Muslims arrived from as far afield as Afghanistan and Africa on the ships which brought immigrants from India, and within the subcontinent itself from diverse regions, ranging from Allahabad to Kashmir. Ibrahim and Alleema were listed as originating from Kabul in Afghanistan when they registered for emigration in 1858. Their ethnic status is confirmed by the distinguishing feature attributed to Ibrahim: a 'yellow complexion'.

As with the Christians, it is certain that Muslims are under-enumerated in the records. Meerah and Cader Rowter of Madura, whose relatives were Shaik Ferreed and Hossein Saib Rowter respectively, were not listed as Muslims but under a caste name of 'Lubbay'. When Moideen Saib and Sheik Muctoom, both aged 30 and from Pondicherry arrived on the *India* in 1858 they were registered not as Muslims but as Malabars. Their next of kin were listed Mahomed Esoof and Sheik Nataud respectively, and there seems little doubt about their Muslim status.

There were both a small number of arriving Indians already in Hindu-Muslim partnerships, and a further number of such unions contracted in Mauritius. Seven of 1,039 married couples arriving in Mauritius were between a Hindu and a Muslim. Interestingly, of ten polygamous unions enumerated in the sample, all involved Hindu men with more than one spouse, rather than Muslims (Carter, 1994: 281). Amongst Indian immigrants marrying in Mauritius five of 165 marriages sampled involved a Muslim woman and a Hindu male, and one was of a Hindu female with a Muslim male. A number of Muslim men intermarried with Christian women: Moosoody married Mari Honorine Brasse at Port Louis in 1876, and Hoomudally Buckus took a Christian Tamil bride, Emeline Samy, in 1874. Nujurally's wife, Marie Cecile Pierbaccasse, was perhaps a converted Muslim. Seetohul Boolaky was listed as a Muslim despite his Hindu first name - he wed Anne Eglée Souza in 1873. Boolaky was from Patna and arrived in Mauritius in 1860.

As with the Hindus, there was considerable solidarity among Muslims of different regional groups in the construction of a religious identity and sites of worship in 19th century Mauritius. Muslim immigrants grouped together to donate land and money for the construction of mosques. In 1884, Eltaup, the son of Dilmohamed, a schoolteacher, resident at Flacq, received a donation of a plot of land, one eighth of an arpent in size, from a group of fellow Muslims, made under the condition 'qu'il existera toujours une mosquée musulmane sur la dite portion de terrain, laquelle mosquée sera toujours ouverte à tous les musulmans généralement, que la dite portion de terrain sera affecté aux besoins de la dite mosquée'.[9] The group of donors on this occasion included Rustum Fakim, a proprietor, based in Pamplemousses, Foondon, a coachman (*carrioleur*), Bugalee and Jeewoollah, two more proprietors from Flacq, and Jeetoo with his wife Joomone. What had brought this group together? They did not come from the same village, they were not even *jehaji bhai*. They had arrived in Mauritius at different times, and had settled on different sugar estates. Jeetoo must have arrived around 1844, judging from his immigrant number, which was 42,381. Bhugalee had migrated with his wife and three children as a 50 year old. His district of origin was the bhojpuri heartland of Arrah in Bihar. Foondon had arrived on the *Thomas Hamlin*, via Calcutta in August 1857. He was then 34 years old, from the village of Pownee in Rezambud. Jewoollah had arrived in 1856 on the *Myaram Dyaram* from Bombay. He may, therefore, have been Marathi speaking. The leader of the group, on whom the plot was conferred, Eltaup, had arrived as a 13 year old on board the *Canning*. He originated from the village of Naugara in the district of Chuprah. In 1878 he completed his term of industrial residence, and settled in Mauritius. He married a Miss Meerally on 13 October 1883 at Flacq. This group of individuals were brought together in Mauritius, and resolved to pool their resources to construct a monument to their faith in the land of their settlement.

In a society composed of disparate ethnic groups, the less influential minorities are bound to disappear in the process of integration into a new society. To date, very little research has been conducted into the various components of the Indian population who migrated to Mauritius from 1834 under the indenture system, and in particular into the numerous linguistic and regional groups which arrived on these shores. This article has demonstrated how new 'communities' were constructed from these diverse elements by the identification of a common ground. Shared religious values and a common 'class' origin provided the essential elements for the creation of such 'communities'. In the process, minorities have been absorbed into larger religious groupings, and the structure of modern Mauritian society was thereby established.

References

1. The sample was obtained from ship registers of arriving immigrants held at the Mahatma Gandhi Institute Immigration Archive (MGI) PE series. All references to ship data included in this article, unless otherwise stated, are held in this collection.
2. MA PA 69 Statements of Marie Cécile 9 March 1885; Luckman 22.2.85; IO notes 26 and 28 Feb 85; PA 70 Insp Gen of Police to PI 19 Mar 1885. The immigration certificates of her relatives are found at MGI PE 75 and PC 825.
3. The data from the ship register PE 71 were corrected in this case by reference to the Married Couple volume for the same ship, PE 65.
4. MA Z4B Vol 6 1877-8 Report of 19.11.1877.
5. Idem, Ducray Report of 26.11.1877.
6. MA RA 2573/1455 Petition of Essoo, 16 March 1880; Minute of Colonial Secretary 18 March; Report of Acting Procureur General 7 April 1880.
7. MA PA Letter of Neyrolles to the Protector of Immigrants 21 March 1907.
8. MA PA 204 IDMP 5 June 1899.
9. MA NA 117/23 PLANEL 1884 24 juin 1884 Désistement par l'Indien Eltaup en faveur de la communauté musulmane.

The Role of Creoles in Chinese Settlement

James Ng Foong Kwong

Chinese immigration to Mauritius is a relatively new field of study, reposing, as it does, on Ly Tio Fane's thesis "Chinese Diaspora in Western Indian Ocean". Her work has served to place this branch of Mauritian history on the agenda by reconstructing, with statistics, the legal and administrative context of this migratory stream. This article takes up a theme which has hitherto not been the focus of detailed study: the crucial support of creole-born British subjects in facilitating the social and economic integration of an alien population - the Chinese - in 19th century Mauritius.

The point of departure in the story of Chinese immigration was the introduction of free Chinese into the colony by the first British governor, Farquhar. In this, he was assisted by the rich Fukienese merchant, Hahime Choisanne, who was to become the first leader or 'Kapitan' of the Chinese in Mauritius. Hahime had been residing in the island since 1816, and was given the authorisation to introduce his compatriots into Mauritius at his own expense. As a result, in 1826, Hahime brought back four Chinese men from a trip to his homeland. They would help to set up the foundations of Chinese commerce in Mauritius. Later, other Chinese joined this little group of traders and it was usually Hahime who acted as their guarantor while they remained in Mauritius. Events in China materially assisted this diaspora. The Opium Wars facilitated out-migration as five ports were opened to foreign trade, namely Canton, Amoy, Fuzhow, Ningpo and Shanghai[1]. It was from these ports, therefore, that the Chinese were able to leave their mother country. Some years later, from 1850, following the Taiping Revolution and the repression of Hakkas which accompanied it, members of this ethnic group also began to leave China (Table 1). Thus, after 1860, the majority of Chinese immigrants arriving in Mauritius were of Hakka origin. Hakka immigration received a boost when the British administration liberalised immigration in 1877. The Hakkas very quickly thereafter outnumbered

Fukienese and Cantonese to become the major component of the Chinese population in Mauritius.

Contemporaneously with free immigration, a number of Chinese contract labourers were introduced into Mauritius. According to Ly Tio Fane, there were in all five attempts to import Chinese labourers to Mauritius between 1760 and 1920. The most important of these was that which occurred between 1840 and 1843, a period coinciding with the prohibition on Indian immigration imposed by the Indian Government (Ly Tio Fane, 1985: 267-280; Carter & Ng, 1997: passim).

Table I : Free Chinese Arriving in Mauritius, 1837 - 1860.

Year	**No. of Chinese**	**Year**	**No. of Chinese**
1837	10	1849	115
1838	12	1850	125
1839	28	1851	48
1840	59	1852	69
1841	59	1853	50
1842	44	1853	50
1843	49	1855	70
1844	64	1856	71
1845	45	1857	118
1846	58	1858	208
1847	62	1859	215
1848	104	1860	379
		Total	2197

Source: H. Ly Tio Fane, *Chinese Diaspora in Western Indian Ocean*, 1985, p.112.

In both the free and contract migratory streams, and as has been the case with other diasporas, it was predominantly men who pioneered the transplantation of Chinese to Mauritius. As Table 2 demonstrates, scarcely any Chinese women were introduced in 19th century Mauritius, and it was not until the beginning of this century that 58 Chinese women arrived in the colony, the first stage of a female immigration which we can chart through the 10 year censuses.

It has been noted elsewhere in this volume that it was through unfree immigration, in fact through slave trading between Asia and the Isle of France, that the first ethnic Chinese were brought. We possess some documentary evidence that these early Sino-Mauritians forged partnerships with other ethnic groups so that families of mixed origin were already in existence in 18th century Isle of France. Further research on the civil status records will bring to light more of these cases, despite the fact that other documents dating from this period are in poor condition.[2] For the British period, petitions and notarial acts permit a more in-depth study of the relationships which developed between Chinese immigrants and local women. It is also possible to follow the careers of the offspring of these partnerships, and to chart the social and economic opportunities open to the Creole-Chinese population at a time when multiculturalism was scarcely dreamt of.

Table 2 : The Chinese Population in Mauritius, 1861 - 1931

Year	Men	Women	Total
1861	1550	2	1552
1871	2284	3	2287
1881	3549	9	3558
1891	3142	9	3151
1901	3457	58	3515
1911	3313	355	3668
1921	5233	1512	1745
1931	6343	2580	6923

Source: *Census Reports 1861-1931.*

Sexual relationships between free men and enslaved women have been a feature of most slave and ex-slave societies, and Mauritius was no exception. Chinese men, like those of other ethnic groups, participated in the common practice of purchasing female slaves who would then serve the dual purpose of concubine and housekeeper. The consensual or forced nature of these relationships is difficult to determine but one of the few ways in which the historian can ascertain the personal bonds which developed is through the enfranchisement and property disposal records.

Men who enfranchised their female slave companions and bestowed property upon them may reasonably be considered to hold some ties of affection to these women and to their children. Of course, in most instances, the paternity of the offspring and the nature of the relationship with the mother, remained unspoken. Thus Ashue, a Chinese man residing in Pamplemousses, merely expressed a wish to enfranchise his Malagasy slave Florine Lop Lop and her three and a half year old daughter, Laurestine. He also undertook to provide food and shelter for Laurestine until she should reach adulthood.[3]

The Chinese immigrants who arrived after the abolition of slavery in mid 19th century Mauritius, whether married or single, like their 18th century male counterparts, commonly filled the lacuna in their emotional life overseas with Coloured and Creole women. These relationships often ended in marriage, but the Chinese were nevertheless criticised for their liaisons with Mauritian females which were considered immoral, and even as a form of prostitution. Mauritian society, in the mid 19th century, was not yet ready to openly accept the notion of couples living together. But there was no doubt also more than a hint of xenophobia in this disapproval (De Rauville, 1908:191). For those Creole women and Chinese men who set up home together, such attitudes could not fail to have an impact on their lives.

For the free or freed Creole women, entering into a relationship with a Chinese man was no doubt an attractive prospect because of the possibilities it opened up for economic mobility in the form of an entree into commerce. A contemporary certainly felt that the ex-apprentice women valued the idea of undertaking a partnership in a small shop as much more attractive than domestic service or field labour:

> *Their feeling (i.e., of emancipated negresses) & opinions of the word "slavery" is so intimately blended with the culture of the soil and the use of the degrading "pioche" that liberty to them must be wholly independent of any field labour whatever (...) They live therefore in hundreds dependent on their husbands, brothers, cousins, &c. and the main repugnance of the black may be attributed to the unceasing efforts on the part of the women in dissuading them from other work than fishing, &c or/what is the acme of their pride/ keeping a shop.*[4]

For some ex-apprentice women, marriage with a Chinese male accordingly gave them access to capital and thereby a chance to launch themselves into the world of petty retail.

For the men concerned, marriage to a Creole was both a means to stabilise their position in Mauritius, and to found a family whose labour was all important in the small business sector. Assam, a Chinese immigrant, freed a slave girl, Adelaide, and subsequently married her. In 1842, he applied to renew his residence permit and requested a licence:

> *The humble petition of Assam no.71 a Chinese resident of many years standing in the colony;*
> *Respectfully sheweth; That your petitioner is legally married to an ex-apprentice whose freedom he purchased many years back.That your petitioner has permission of residence until the end of this year;That your petitioner is anxious of obtaining the same favor for the approaching year, also permission to take out a license...*[5]

Evidently Adelaide took an active part in the business, for at the same time she drafted a petition of her own asking for the renewal of her shop licence.[6]

Creole women were British subjects, and the Chinese believed that marriage with them would facilitate the regularisation of their own status and their administrative dealings with the local government. In a report dated 19 October 1843, the Commissioner of Police noted

> *That no Chinaman can obtain a license from the Internal Revenue Office except under a special authority from H.E the Governor upon petitions reported upon from this office.*[7]

It was thus, in many cases, the creole wife who would undertake to request the shop licence needed. As Marie Françoise, wife of the Chinese immigrant Acome, explained in her petition:

> *That your petitioner having the intention to open a shop in Corderie street most humbly sollicit Your Excellency's permission to grant her a license to sell wine, beer and sweet liquors in her own name; as your petitioner having learnt that her husband being a stranger in the colony was not allowed to carry on business in his own name.....*[8]

Once the licence was granted, the Chinese husband and his relatives or acquaintances could be employed in the business, thus enabling the immigrants to obtain residence permits and a backdoor entry into commerce in the colony. Naturally, this did not long escape the attention of the local police. In 1843, they noted that 56 licences had been granted to Chinese immigrants, and a further 11 to the Creole wives or partners of Chinese men.[9] The local authorities were consequently on the alert for evidence of marriages which were deemed to have been transacted for the primary purpose of facilitating the business affairs of Chinese men. In May 1845 the Chief Commissary of Police reported having failed to confirm the request for a shop licence made by one Mrs Amine. He explained his decision as follows:

> *Early in the present month the usual declaration for a shop license was presented for my signature under the name of Mrs Amine and on questioning the female who brought it she stated that she was the wife of a Chinese of that name, and produced a document from which it appeared that she was little more than 14 years of age and had been married only on the 7th instant evidently with the intention to obtain a shop licence.* [10]

Amine had arrived in Mauritius on 7 September 1844 and since that time was believed to have been employed 'in some of his countrymen's shops'. To end any further 'abuse' of the law, Ordinance 27 of 1845 was passed which stipulated that:

> *toute patente autre qu'une patente de colportage sera délivrée sous le nom de la personne voulant exercer le commerce, la profession, l'art ou le métier y désignés et ne pourra être transférée ni confiée à aucun agent ou représentant d'une autre personne, qui ne serait pas expressément nommée dans ladite patente...*[11]

Because of this law Cécilia Affoy, a Creole, upon renewing her licence, requested that the name of her husband be added to it:

> *The petition of Mrs. Cécilia Affoy, humbly sheweth -That Your Excellency was pleased to grant her a first class shop license for the year 1847 & desirous to continue her trade, she therefore sollicits that Your Excellency will be pleased to grant*

the same favor for the year 1848, also to allow her to put her husband name Affoy in her shop during her absence.....[12]

Those women who were ignorant of this law, or chose to flout it, soon fell foul of the new measures which provided for fines of up to £20 for the clandestine employment of immigrants. The wife of Amine, for example, was fined £2, and later, when she attempted to renew her licence, and to include her husband's name, the authorities categorically refused.

As the number of shops being run by Chinese immigrants increased, pressure was placed on the authorities by local shopholders and merchants to clamp down on Chinese boutique owners. By 1847, greater vigilance was being exercised by the Commissioner of Police with regard to the granting of licences to Creole women; new requests were systematically rejected, and renewals became increasingly difficult. Aware of the complicity which had developed between these women and the Chinese immigrants, the Commissioner bluntly rejected the permit of Christine Ahong on 17 November 1847, with the words:

Christine Ahong is a Creole of the colony married to a Chinese. I cannot recommend any more shops to be kept by Chinese.[13]

It was primarily economic motives - the concern about competition - which led to this clampdown. Yet, it was certainly true that in some cases the permits were entirely fictitious, in that the Creole woman was simply lending her name to a small business which was effectively being run by a Chinese man. Thus, in refusing a permit requested by Marie Elisara, the Commissioner demonstrated his doubts about her role:

Marie Elisara prays to be allowed to renew her shop license - This license actually belongs to the Chinese Avoine so that it is a mere 'Pretnom'. Nothing is however known against the woman.[14]

Of course, the suspicions of the authorities inevitably hindered the legitimate business interests of Creole women whose existing contacts with the Chinese community, even to the extent of familiarising themselves with the Chinese language, naturally predisposed them to take on other Chinese as employees. Louise Marie Jeanne Ally, who wished to employ three Chinese immigrants, was initially refused permission to do so purely on the grounds that she was a Creole. Persisting in her request, she explained to the Governor that this refusal would affect the running of her two shops:

> *That the three Chinamen Among No. 419, Atchoon No.507 and Igloo No.267 have been especially recommended to your petitioner by her husband as honest and able clerks;*
>
> *That your petitioner wishes to employ so many as three clerks it is because by virtue of the authorisation which your Excellency has been pleased to give her, she intends to keep two shops and wants her customers to be well and quickly served.*
>
> *That the wives of other Chinamen have already, as well as your Petitioner was before this refusal, been authorised to employ Chinamen as their clerks, and there exists no cause why your petitioner should not be granted the same favour.*
>
> *That from her marriage, the Chinese language has become familiar to your petitioner, and it is much more convenient for her to be assisted and served by Chinamen than by Indians whose language she does not understand.*[15]

Following this second petition, the Commissioner of Police allowed her to take on two of the three Chinese she wished to employ. Another would-be employer was Dame Pierre Renaud, who, in 1849, requested to employ a Chinese named Quequene as a clerk in her shop. She was also refused permission. Creole women were certainly in many cases more than just convenient names. They could also use their own property as a security: Delphine Catherine, the wife of Ayou, a Chinese trader, was able to borrow 164 *piastres* from V. Sinnatambou by mortgaging her three plots of land of 9 arpents in size located near Pieter Both. When Ahine, a rich merchant, bought a schooner, the *Emma,* at public auction, it was Victorine Paris, a shopkeeper, who bailed him out of a difficult situation by registering the vessel in her name.[16]

Thus, and despite the best efforts of the local police, a report drawn up in June 1849 revealed that Chinese immigrants were continuing to benefit from the assistance of Creole women to launch themselves in commercial ventures in Mauritius. Creole men also assisted Chinese traders in the running of their businesses. The Chinese Kapitan, Hahime, also benefited from a close working relationship with Mauritians of other ethnic groups: he worked closely with Alfred Lagesse in the management of his business, whilst the Chinese Jean Shoon set up a company with one J. Ulysse. In 1840 Assian was charged with running a shop which was however licenced to one Auguste Sophie. Sophie was a painter by trade and was considered by the colonial administration 'not a likely person to keep a shop, or put any person in one on his account, but has lent his name, a thing very common to the Chinamen to obtain, but generally in the name of a female'.[17]

Creole-Chinese Family Relationships

Despite the opposition expressed in Mauritian society to relationships between Creole women and Chinese men, many couples did form lasting relationships, founding families and overcoming religious and cultural obstacles to take their place in 'respectable' society. Marriage was in some cases simply a means to formalise and legitimise the offspring of a long term relationship. Thus Ahine decided to wed Victorine Petulente, mother of his two children, in 1846, on the eve of a long voyage to Singapore, Penang and other Eastern ports. Ahine was already a naturalised British subject, and before his departure he drew up an 'acte de procuration' in which he named two Chinese men, natives of Pekin like himself, to assist his wife with the running of his 8 shops in Port Louis. Ahine was not thinking simply of business; he was also acting as a family man, and to cover for his absence, he delegated the primary responsibility for his dependants to his Creole wife:

> *Et donner en outre à sa dite épouse tous les pouvoirs de gérer & administrer les affaires qui concernent leur communauté de biens & l'intérieur de leur mariage.*[18]

The wives in these family groups not only participated actively in the management of the shops, but being in many cases literate, were able to give precious assistance to their husbands in their correspondence and administrative dealings. Elise Athion, wife of one of the earliest Chinese immigrants, was a model member of this group. She held two licences, one for the sale of food and the other for soft drinks. Successfully combining the running of her shops with the raising of her children, she and her family rose from humble beginnings, to gain admittance to the inner circle of rich and influential members of the Chinese community in 19th century Mauritius.

It is interesting to note that the sons of these early Creole-Chinese families were by and large raised according to Chinese traditions, whilst the daughters tended to follow the customs of their mothers. Thus boys were given Chinese first names, wore their hair in a pig tail and dressed in Chinese garments whilst girls wore European style clothes, were baptised and given a Christian education. For example, Changuan's Creole-Chinese daughters were named Diandia and Marie Amelie, whilst his son was given the Chinese name Sing Sive. As de Rauville wrote:

> *les filles sont élevées d'après les usages créoles, et les garçons selon les coutumes chinoises; de bonne heure ceux-ci portent le chapeau de paille, le large pantalon, la camisole de soie et les babouches aux hautes semelles de carton; on laisse croître leurs cheveux, et à neuf ans on commence à les tresser en natte. Ils apprennent la langue paternelle qui est interdite aux filles.* (De Rauville, 1908: 191).

Despite their westernized education, the young Creole-Chinese girls were actively sought after as marriage partners by Chinese merchants or young Sino-Mauritian men. As the legal age of marriage in Mauritius in the 19th century was 15, the Governor was frequently requested to allow girls of 13 or 14 to marry. Thus Athon petitioned that his 14 year old daughter Marie Amelie be allowed to marry Angtioky:

> *A l'honneur d'exposer bien respectueusement Athon Chinois, marchand demeurant en cette ville de Port Louis;*
>
> *Que ma fille Marie Amélie Athon, née de son légitime mariage avec Elisa Cote Destré aujourd'hui décédée, est recherchée en mariage par Angtioky, mais que l'exposant n'a pu obtenir de*

l'officier de l'Etat Civil de Port Louis de faire afficher ce mariage parce que d'après l'acte de naissance ci-inclus de Marie Amélie, sa fille, cette dernière n'aurait que quatorze ans et six mois, tandis que d'après l'article 144 du Code Civil, il faut que la femme ait quinze ans accomplis pour pouvoir contracter mariage.

L'exposant vient en conséquence solliciter qu'il vous plaise, Excellence,

vouloir bien user en faveur de sa fille des pouvoirs que vous sont conférés par l'article 145 du même Code Civil, en lui accordant la dispense d'âge voulu par la loi pour qu'elle puisse contracter mariage....[19]

Both Creole and Creole-Chinese women played an important part in the religious organisation of the mixed household. According to H. Ly Tio Fane, this strong influence propelled the majority of the Chinese community to embrace a Christian faith.

> *Si le père insistait pour que les enfants, particulièrement les fils, soient élevés dans la tradition, et instruits dans la langue chinoise, la mère se faisait un devoir de baptiser tous ses enfants et de les élever dans la religion chrétienne (...) La fidélité des femmes envers leur religion fit rapidement augmenter le nombre de catholiques dans la communauté chinoise.* (Ly Tio Fane, 1985: 281).

The authorities also remarked upon this trend towards conversion to Catholicism, at the beginning of the present century, for betwen the census dates of 1901 and 1911 the number of Chinese Catholics had more than doubled: from 203 in 1901 to 520 in 1911. They stated as follows:

> *Un changement majeur apparaît parmi les membres de la communauté chinoise qui tendent à se convertir, particulièrement au catholicisme, cela est évidemment dû à la présence d'un certain nombre de femmes créoles parmi eux, ou du moins de femmes de sang mêlé, mais il faut aussi compter des conversions.* [20]

Hahime Choisanne and his relationships with Creole women

It was important to raise the male child in Creole-Chinese families with an understanding of Chinese traditions, because it was he who would assure the continuity of the family lineage. Male children were not baptised, and were expected to follow their fathers' customs. This would stand them in good stead in case of an eventual return to China. The training given by fathers to sons in Chinese language and customs, is shown in the case of the natural child of Hahime Choisanne. Hahime's relationship with Eléonore Curaux led to the birth of a son named Tianne Fate. The boy was given a Chinese manservant, and when he was old enough, was sent to live in China. He returned from time to time to Mauritius to visit his parents. Due to his circumstances, Tianne Fate, like other Chinese, was considered to be an 'alien' by the authorities, rather than a native of the island. In this way, Tianne Fate grew up divorced from the Creole milieu into which he had been born. Hahime, in Mauritius, meanwhile took another mistress, in the person of Eléonore Julie. [21]

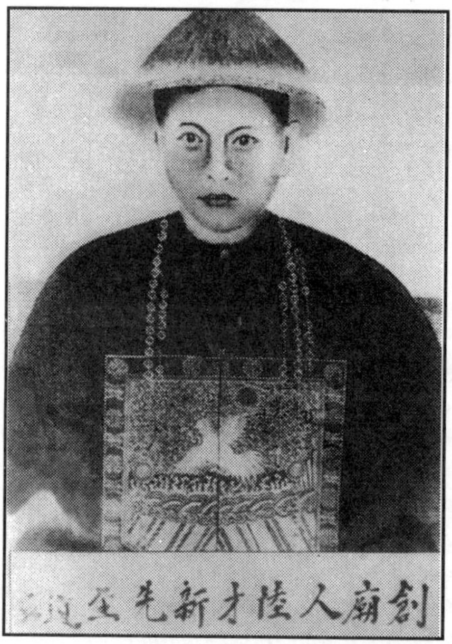

Hahime, the First Chinese Kapitan

Despite his distance from his son, and his other relationships, Hahime Choisanne considered the boy his sole inheritor, and, concerned, like other businessmen, to bequeath his fortune appropriately, he made numerous wills during his lifetime, between 1837 and his eventual departure from Mauritius around 1872.[22] It was during a slight illness, in July 1837, that Hahime first called for the notary to visit his residence in Royal Road, Port Louis, and established the details of his closest relatives:

> *Je n'ai qu'un seul enfant nommé Tianne Fate de mes liaisons avec Eléonore Curaux. Je n'ai d'ailleurs aucun autre dépendant ni aucun ascendant. J'ai un frère établi à Pulopinan nommé Atche, boulanger - et un neveu établi à Canton nommé Kane Faye menuisier appelé Quaïssing ou Faïssing.*

Hahime planned to bequeath his entire fortune to his son, capital which amounted to two food shops, one at the bazar and another at Royal Road. To manage these two shops, Hahime named two Chinese, Fancyone or Fon-Youne and Manhin as his executors. He wished his son to be brought up in China, and made the following arrangements:

> *Mes exécuteurs testamentaires feront après ma mort ce qu'ils croiront le plus convenable aux intérêts de mon fils. Ils conserveront les boutiques si bon leur semble, et si la chose est possible, ou ils les vendront. Et les ventes réalisées mon désir est qu'ils ammènent mon fils à Canton dans sa famille à laquelle, ils remettraient en même temps le produit des ventes ainsi que toutes les valeurs qui composeraient ma succession.*

The will he made in 1851 introduced several important changes. As his son was by then living in China, he instructed his new executors, Ackine and Ahene, to realise the assets from his shops and to send the resulting capital to his son. He bequeathed a small property in Moka to the woman he currently lived with, Eléonore Julie. He had bought this property in 1844, and it was worth around 250 *piastres*.

A further modification Hahime made to his will was to prove of significance to the entire Chinese population of the island: he bequeathed the Coan-Tahi-Biou, better known today as the Salines or Kwan Tee Pagoda, to the community at large.

> *Je déclare en outre que le terrain en cette ville, près du Camp des Salines, par moi acquis et où est édifié la chapelle des Chinois, ne m'appartient pas personnellement, qu'il est la propriété de tous les Chinois en cette île professant le même culte que moi, pour l'usage auquel il est actuellement destiné.*

Bequests of Chinese traders

The wills left by other Chinese immigrants reveal their divided loyalties. Many dreamt of a definitive return to the mother country once they had amassed sufficient capital. In the meantime they paid frequent visits to China, distributing their wealth amongst their relatives and making contacts with Asian merchants. Their ties to Mauritius were equally strong: it was here that they made their money and where they had founded new families. The wills of these Chinese immigrants clearly demonstrate the dispersal of their human ties: most were written in a spirit of equity - the dependants in China and in Mauritius were all recognised as beneficiaries.

For those Chinese who had no family in Mauritius, most of their wealth was repatriated, save for donations made to the pagoda where they worshipped in the colony. The will of Atchowan, drawn up on 6 April 1858, is typical. His brother Anthoo, also resident in Mauritius, was given a small bequest; the rest of his fortune was divided between his relatives in China:

> *Je donne et lègue à Agouan, ma mère résidant en Chine, pour la remplir de ses droits dans ma succession la somme de quatre cents piastres (...), à Atchoa, ma soeur, résidant actuellement en Chine, la somme de trois cents piastres (...), à Isywat, mon frère, résidant actuellement en Chine, la somme de cinq cents piastres, à Anthoo, mon frère, demeurant au Port Louis, la somme de deux cents piastres.*
>
> *Je donne et lègue à l'église chinoise établie en cette île, rue Versailles la somme de quatre cents piastres. Pour ladite somme être remise au chef de ladite église aussitôt la liquidation de ma succession.*[23]

Those with families in Mauritius generally made provision for these latter alongside their relatives in China. The will of Changuan, also known as Chang Goine, demonstrates the spirit of equality with which the fortune was divided:

> *Je ne laisse aucun ascendant ni descendant légitime. Je donne et lègue à la Delle. Julia et à mes enfants naturels Diandia née le vingt huit août mil huit cent quarante sept, Marie Amélie née*

le vingt sept mai mil huit cent quarante neuf et Sing Sive né le dix neuf août mil huit cent cinquante un, tous trois mineurs, issus de mes liaisons avec ladite Delle. Julia, et à chacun pour un quart, tout le contenu, sans exception aucune, en une boutique de comestibles tenue par Mr. Diotine en un pavillon en bois appartenant à Mr. Adolphe Pamphile sus-nommé situé en cette ville au Camp de L'Est, sur la route des Pamplemousses et portant le no.38.

Je donne et lègue à mes neveux et nièces en Chine enfants de Mouy, mon frère décédé tout le contenu sans exception en une boutique de comestibles et spiritueux tenue par M. Dishune dans un pavillon en bois appartenant à Mde. Ve. Amire Mamedi situé en cette ville au Camp de l'Est sur la route des Pamplemousses et patentée sous le no. 1314.[24]

The Chinese nephews and nieces who inherited his goods were in effect being bequeathed a business opportunity and an invitation to migrate. Surely, many came to Mauritius in this manner, and one can only speculate what might have been their contacts with their Creole-Chinese relatives in Mauritius.

It was customary for testators to appoint another Chinese man as their executor, despite the fact that their Creole spouse was in many cases still alive. The executor would usually have been the confidant of the will maker, a person known to be a good businessman and someone who moved in the same circles. The role of the executor was not simply to make known the wishes of the deceased but to settle debts and realise assets. Thus Angounne, a Chinese trader of Royal Road, Port Louis, nominated Assene as an executor and stipulated that he should manage his goods in the best interest of his Creole wife and their son. Three hundred *piastres* were set aside for the deceased's parents in China:

Ce qui restera de mes biens sera réalisé et je laisse à ma femme sous la direction de mon exécuteur testamentaire ci-après nommé le soin de le placer soit par prêts sur bonnes garanties hypothécaires, soit dans l'acquisition d'immeubles. Ma femme aura la jouissance des rentes produites par ces placements de fonds, ou de loyers des maisons qu'elle pourra acquérir jusqu' à la majorité de mon fils Ahan.[25]

The executor would himself often be remunerated for the responsibilities which he undertook, particularly when the guardianship of minor children was involved, in order to ensure that the sons be educated in Chinese fashion:

> *Je nomme Assène marchand chinois, mon ami, pour mon exécuteur testamentaire (....) et pour l'indemniser des peines qu'il prendra pour surveiller les affaires de ma succession et exécuter mes volontés je lui abandonne et lègue trois pour cent sur le produit net de ma dite succession. Je désire aussi que ledit Assène soit nommé le subrogé-tuteur de mon fils Ahan....*

The Marriage of Affan Tank Wen, Second Chinese Kapitan: A Symbol of Integration

The testaments described above testify to the importance of Creoles to the Chinese men who settled in Mauritius. Hahime, the Kapitan or head of the Chinese in Mauritius and spiritual leader of the community, had evidently not suffered any loss in status as a result of living with a Creole woman. Nor did Affan Tank Wen, his successor, who married a Creole-Chinese and was baptised. Quite the contrary, he combined with ease his position as spiritual leader of the Chinese and his philanthropic activities within the Catholic Church, working with Mother Barthelemy, known as 'la Mère des Pauvres'.

In fact the event of 12 June 1872, when Affan Tank Wen wed Marie Elizabeth Athow, is probably the best known example of a marriage between a Creole-Chinese woman and a Chinese immigrant. In so doing, Affan Tank Wen became one of the first Chinese to convert to Catholicism in order to marry a Christian woman.

Affan Tank Wen had arrived in Mauritius on 31 August 1861, at the age of 19. The son of Tank Wen and Honsy, he began his career overseas as an employee of the commercial house of 'Achim et Cie'. His hard work, loyalty and savoir faire led to his promotion to Director of the firm. He amassed a large personal fortune, became an active member of the Chamber of Commerce and was recognised as one of the most popular members of the community. On his baptism in 1872, he took the name of Louis. Henceforth he was to lead a religious double life. On the one hand, he helped to build a Chinese pagoda dedicated to the divinity Hon T'U and participated in meetings held therein. On the other hand, he played an active part, along with Mother Barthelemy in converting Chinese to Catholicism, contributed financially to the Bon Secours Convent and to the Chinese Hospital which the sisters ran, and erected a monument to her at the Western Cemetery. His work to assist members of the community in distress, and his contribution to good causes such as the foundation of a Plague Hospital in 1899 earned him the title 'Protector of the Poor'. He made an incursion into politics in 1882 to publicise his views on constitutional change, and following the adoption of the 1886 constitution he was elected leader of the Chinese community. He died on 2 June 1900 (Nagapen, 1991: 47-50).

Emile Athion: the lifestyle of a Creole-Chinese

For those who grew up in Mauritius, and were more exposed to the cultural heritage of both parents, it was possible to take on a dual identity. Some boys were baptised like their mothers, but were nevertheless exposed to the Confucian principles of their fathers. The new generation of Creole-Chinese proved to be as assiduous in pursuing commercial success as their Chinese born fathers had been. Emile Athion promoted the ideals of his Chinese father from within a Creole society. The son of Marie Lourdes and her Chinese husband Athion, Emile grew up in an atmosphere of tolerance, exposed to both religious influences. Emile was baptised into the Anglican faith. He became known as a social activist, helping new Chinese immigrants to settle in Mauritius, offering them work, and acting as a guarantor in their dealings with the colonial administration. Inevitably, this led to friction with the police authorities who thought he was encouraging immigration by employing excessive numbers of Chinese workers. In 1849 he was refused permission to employ another clerk:

> *Emile Athion has already two or three clerks in his shop. I cannot recommend his having any more.*[26]

Because he was a Creole and a British subject, Emile, like his mother, was able to provide assistance to Chinese immigrants. Being fluent in both his paternal and in European languages, he was able to play an important role within the nascent Cantonese community in Mauritius. The importance of Emile Athion for the Cantonese community is shown by the following request addressed by him to the Governor, asking for a pagoda for this group. Dated 1 February 1861, the letter indicates why Emile was chosen as the spokesman for the Cantonese in Mauritius:

> *The absence of a chapel where Chinese from Macao, (who speak a different language and are of a different caste from the other Chinese) can practise their religion, having been felt, I have on many occasions, been applied to, to solicit from His Excellency the Governor the authority to establish a chapel for them. The reason why they have addressed themselves to me is because I am a Creole Chinese born in this island, and enjoying all the rights and privileges of a British subject.*
>
> *As there seems to exist some difficulty as to whether any place dedicated to divine worship may be open to the public without His Excellency's sanction, I have the honor to solicit most respectfully His Excellency's authority for establishing a chapel for the benefit of the Chinese from Macao.*[27]

Permission was given, on condition that the pagoda did not undertake any activities which would threaten public order. This warning was no doubt linked to an incident which had occurred in the pagoda founded by Hahime, having been transformed into a gambling den. When the police raided the building and tried to arrest the players, some fatalities had occurred. [28]

At the same time as assisting the Cantonese community, Emile Athion was also undertaking Christian acts of charity. He was reputed for his benevolent acts in favour of the poor, and took care of a godchild, a Creole orphan named Marie Emile. In 1860 he petitioned the governor to enable her to marry the Chinese trader Chankin Mon.[29] He died on 19 April 1867 in Pamplemousses, mourned by the Mauritian Cantonese community.

His son, Louis Emilien Athion, was to demonstrate even closer ties to the Anglican community into which his father had been inducted. In 1879 he petitioned the Governor for permission to change his name into that of Smith. Born in 1859, Louis was the acknowledged natural child of Emile Athion and of Josephine Eleonore Dumont. Evidently, the boy was brought up by an English family, for his petition declared:

> *That your petitioner during his tender age was cared for by one Mr George Smith which fact caused your Petitioner to be known under the family name of Smith which name he still bears and is known under. That your petitioner is desirous of having his family name of Athion changed into that of Smith.* [30]

Adrien Konfortion: the myth shattered

The Creole-Chinese have often been perceived as second class in relation to the families where both parents are of Chinese origin, leading Ly Tio Fane to comment that 'children of mixed marriage, raised in the Mauritian Culture did not achieve great success as traders, nor did they usually succeed their father in the managerial role' (Ly Tio Fane: 1995). In fact, research has itself already revealed the hollowness of these stereotypes.

Ly Tio Fane has demonstrated that A Konfortion, himself a Creole-Chinese, was not only a successful manager at the heart of the well known commercial house of Ng Cheng Hin, but also occupied the post of Secretary of the Chinese Chamber of Commerce for 29 years. During these years, he proved himself to be a skilful intermediary between the Chinese community and the colonial administration (Ly Tio Fane, 1985: 331-333). [42]

Born in Quartier Militaire, Mauritius, in 1882, the son of a Chinese immigrant and a Mauritian mother, Elmida Allot, Adrien Konfortion grew up in Bois Clair, near the sugar estate of Sans Souci where his parents ran a shop. When he was 18 years old, Adrien accompanied his parents to China where he spent two years. Back in Mauritius in 1903, and having acquired a mastery of the Hakka language, he was able to put his trilingualism to good use. Working for Ng Cheng Hin, he ordered goods directly from Europe and helped that firm to achieve local prominence.

His skill in negotiation propelled him to a position of spokesman for the Chinese in Mauritius and he was also directly involved with procedures for new arrivals in the colony. In 1926 he married Lucie Affoy, a Catholic like himself. His social role was further enlarged by his work for Chinese youth and his collaboration in the setting up of the Chinese Hospital in 1921. In 1946 the Governor of the island, Sir Donald Mackenzie-Kennedy, proposed him to represent the Chinese community in the Legislative Council, an offer which he refused. He died in 1956, aged 74 (Nagapen, 1991: 50-52).

This article has sought to re-evaluate the role of Creoles, and particularly Creole women, in the implantation of the Chinese community in Mauritius. The relationships which grew up between Creoles and Chinese have been misunderstood and denigrated by contemporaries and historians alike. In fact, as this article has demonstrated, Creole women played a crucial role in the commercial success of their male partners, acting as their representatives and spokeswomen in their contacts with the colonial authorities. These families and their descendants proved to be of great importance both in assisting the immigration of Chinese and in contributing to the development of commerce. If the sons of these families tended to be favoured as the recipients and transmitters of Chinese culture, the daughters were also integrated into the Chinese community through marriage. Creole-Chinese men like Emile Athion and Adrien Konfortion, through their multilingual abilities and managerial skills, and above all their status as British subjects, occupied important posts at the heart of the Chinese community and were respected mediators for the Chinese-speaking traders. In an ironic footnote to the history of Chinese immigration, a group classed, despite its distinctiveness, in the 'General Population' came, in fact, to depend very greatly on this larger social category.

References

1. The Treaty of Nankin in 1842 imposed this condition on the Chinese.
2. See, for example, the discussion of the civil status documents as shedding light on the incidence of mixed marriages in the first article of this volume.
3. MA NA 91/7 'Obligation par Ashue Chinois en faveur de Laurestine Lop Lop son affranchie', 6 oct 1828.
4. PRO CO 167/226 Letter of J.A. Lloyd to John Irving, 4 April 1840.
5. MA RA 711 Petition of Assam (no.71), 22 December 1842.
6. MA RA 711 Petition of Adélaïde Assam, 28 December 1842.
7. MA RA 59 Report of Commissary of Police, 19 October 1843.
8. MA RA 711 Petition of Marie Françoise, wife of Acome, 15 December 1842.
9. MA RA 59 Report of Commissary of Police.
10. MA RA 798 Petition of Amine, 14 May 1845.
11. MA B3B, 1844-1850, p.77.
12. MA RA 938 Petition of Cécilia Affoy, 10 November 1847.
13. MA RA 938 Report of Commissary of Police, 17 November 1847.
14. MA RA 938 Report relative to petition of Marie Elisara, 13 November 1847.
15. MA RA 984 Petition of Louise Marie Jeanne Ally, 30 December 1848.
16. MA RB 197 Colonial Secretary to Chief Commissary of Police, 15 June 1849; NA 92/3 'Obligation par M & Mme Ayou au profit de M. Sinnatambou', 6 juillet 1884; RA 775 Collector of Customs to Colonial Secretary, 2 December 1844.
17. MA RA 606 Finniss to Col Secy, 5 May 1840; Ng, 1996: 51-2; 250.
18. MA NA 82/6/2210 Procuration d'Ahine, 2 mars 1847.
19. MA RA 1035 Petition of Athon, 17 January 1849
20. MA Census Report, 1911.
21. MA NA 78/18/4074 Testament d'Hahime Choisanne, 19 juillet 1837.

22. MA NA 78/18/4047 Testament d'Hahime Choisanne, 19 juillet 1837; NA 75/37/234 Testament d'Hahime Choisanne, 24 mars 1851.

23. MA NA 94/21/2914-94 Testament du Chinois Atchowan, 6 avril 1858.

24. MA NA 94/1 Testament de Changuan ou Chang Goine, 19 mars 1852.

25. MA NA 78/21/2067 Testament d'Angounne, 13 avril 1838.

26. MA RA 1035/2441 Petition of Emile Athion, 16 February 1849.

27. MA RA 1619 Petition of Emile Athion, 1 February 1861.

28. Idem.

29. MA RA 1573 Petition of Emile Athion, 15 March 1860.

30. MA RA 2507 Petition of Louis Emilien Athion, 28 November 1879.

Recapturing the African Past: 19th Century Afro-Creole Genealogies

Marina Carter

The African presence in Mauritius is generally consigned to the drawer marked slavery. Yet there were princes, ambassadors, *marmittes,* contract workers, sailors, and liberated apprentices amongst the number of visitors from that continent to these shores. The aim of this article is to shed light on the arrival of Africans in Mauritius in the post-abolition period and to trace their subsequent settlement on the island, through two case studies. The Lily and Koomanikooa families descend from hundreds of Africans rescued from slaving vessels in the Indian Ocean and 'liberated' into apprenticeships which they served in Mauritius between 1840 and 1870. The following accounts of the integration of these individuals into Mauritian society provide a further dimension to the search for African 'roots' and an African heritage, and trace the process through which African identities have merged into an Afro-Creole community.

Evolving Identities: HMS Lily and her African Passengers

HMS Lily was a 169 ton brig built by Symonds which did active service as a British Royal Navy Cruiser in the Indian Ocean during the first half of the 19th century.[1] Under Commander Seymour, the brig carried out an action in 1840 which led to the foundation of the Lily colony at Mauritius. It is that story which concerns us here. Britain's anti slave trade laws and treaties provided for the capture of vessels engaged in unauthorised trading in slaves, and their condemnation as prizes. The slaves 'liberated' from such ships were taken to settlements created for their reception on the African mainland, as at Freetown, Sierra Leone, or were sent to serve terms of apprenticeship in British colonies. At times of labour shortage, the manpower available from such 'apprentices' was highly sought after. In 1840 Mauritius was sorely in need of workers to meet the expansion of sugar cultivation. Prices of sugar were high, but Indian immigration was temporarily suspended. In April of that year, the Secretary of State for the Colonies in London gave orders to the Commander of *HMS Lily* to send 'any slave vessels captured on or near the Mozambique Channel' to Mauritius, so that those on board could be distributed as apprentices to the Mauritian planters.[2]

On 21 June 1840, the *Lily* arrived at Port Louis with 265 Africans on board, saved from the wreck of a Portuguese brig, the *José,* chased on shore off Guillimaine River. The Governor reported, 'so large a number of persons in so small a vessel necessarily exposed the officers and crew to great inconvenience and had exhausted all their provisions and water by the time the Lily reached Mauritius'. Smallpox broke out on board the ship, and 59 of the 324 Africans saved from the wreck of the *José* died en route to the island. Colonel Power then administering the Government caused the *Lily* to be furnished with provisions and water, and had measures promptly taken for providing accommodation for the Africans who had to be kept in quarantine. On the 26th June, all on board were transferred to two hulks hired for the purpose, under the charge of a Medical Officer and the protection of some Police Guards. The Collector of Customs was placed in charge of provisions and clothing supplied to the quarantined Africans.[3]

On the following day, the Medical Officer stationed on the quarantine hulks reported that 'many of his patients were in a low and sinking state'. Ten pounds of beef was sent on board to supplement their daily rations. By August plans were being made to draw up indentures for the Africans, the majority of whom were children. The Collector of Cusoms advised 'additional precautions being taken on account of the utter helplessness of these individuals whatever their age, and because of their liability to oppression and imposition'. He proposed that children under 11 should be apprenticed for 7 years, those aged 11-12 for 6 years, those aged 12-13 for 5 years, 13-14 year olds for 4 years and those aged above 14 for 3 years.

The Africans were not all as helpless as the Collector believed, for in November 1840 he reported that some of them had deserted the services of the persons with whom they were placed: 'one of the deserters was discovered after a day or two in the canes some miles from the place of his master's residence, and in the other case the individual was brought to his master in Port Louis having been found on the highway near the village of Pamplemousses'. Several, however, still remained in hospital, not having yet recovered from their traumatic sea voyage. [4]

By February 1841, 168 of the Africans arrived on the *Lily* had been sent to their new employers, 17 had died in hospital and four at their employers' establishments. One person remained in hospital. More than half of these individuals were less than 11 years old; many were under 7 years old and in consequence the Collector of Customs reported that he considered them 'unable to perform field labour' and distributed them as domestic servants. Fifty of the Africans were given over to government officers, 34 to merchants and private individuals, 15 to tradesmen, 7 to teachers and 78 to planters and to the Botanic Garden. In the selection of employers, wrote Cunningham, the Collector:

> *I have been guided either by their good treatment of former apprentices, or by strong recommendation, or finally by my own knowledge of the worth and humanity of the individuals .. I am led to hope and expect that besides being trained as good and useful subjects, a great proportion of them will be so far educated as to be able to read and write before the expiry of the second year of their apprenticeships.* [5]

Whatever Cunningham's motivations in distributing the young Africans to officials and merchants, many of British origin, it was a fact that at the time of the arrival of HMS Lily, labour was at a premium in Mauritius, and Lord Russell, Secretary of State for the Colonies, had expressly stated that any arriving Africans should be distributed to the planters. The Governor, now called to account for the Collector's proceedings, disclaimed any responsibility in the proceedings, but commented: 'I am not disposed to call in question the integrity of the Collector's intentions or proceedings; nor considering the youth of the large majority of the Africans, to suppose that the planters have lost much by not having obtained their services. But I do think that deference was due from him to your Lordship's instructions, and that they should have been obeyed and carried out fully'. The Governor was more concerned that the wages which the Collector had arranged to bank for the Africans might 'militate against their good treatment and lead to the utmost degree of attainable labour being required from them'. He also felt that the period of indentures was too lengthy. Back in London the Colonial Office criticised the considerable delay that had occurred in organising the indentures.[6]

For some of the young Africans, however, it was the start of a life in the households of some of the most important British officials in the colony, during which apprenticeships a few would journey to England, to India and to Australia. In January 1842, for example, the Chief Judge, James Wilson, applied for leave to allow two of his apprentices to accompany his wife home:

> *As Mrs Wilson and my family are on the eve of leaving this island for England on temporary absence, and propose to take with them 2 young Mozambiques Henry Lily Yamba and Helen Lily Marckennengee, who on 2 Oct 1840 were apprenticed to me for 7 years by you as Collector of HM Customs of this Island, I shall be obliged to you for permission to send my said 2 apprentices to England with Mrs Wilson and my family.*

This was sanctioned, with the proviso that security for the return of the apprentices be given. In April of the same year, the Acting Governor himself asked to take his own apprentice to Britain as a servant. Some of the young Africans went abroad for even longer periods than the several months' leave of absence usually accorded to colonial officials. In November, Mr R Tapley, about to proceed with his wife and family to settle in South Australia, applied to take their 11 year old female apprentice with them 'as the girl is very useful to my wife and child, and herself desirous to remain with us'. Mr Tapley offered testomonies as to 'the general kindness with which the girl is treated in my family', and the Acting Collector recommended the request, 'having satisfied myself that the girl is willing to accompany the parties and having every reason to believe that she will be properly treated'. In March 1845, Pat Lily Pandoo went with his employer, David Richardson, on a trip to Calcutta, and in February 1846, Lionel Lily Joaquin was offered the chance to travel to England in the service of the Queen's Proctor, Mr Ferguson. The Collector wrote 'the boy seems most willing to accompany his master and ... I am convinced that the arrangement will be of great advantage to him'.[7]

Not all of the apprentices were able to benefit from foreign travel and from the above average wages which they earned. Aurore Lily Moupirlla was very ill in hospital for most of 1845. The girl, then aged 18, was reported to be suffering from 'a chronic disease of the skin, and a disease of the bone'. In January 1846, Aurore's employer, Théodore Giblot Ducray, visited her in hospital and reported 'je l'ai trouvé dans le même etat et même dépérissante'. He was advised that her condition would not permit her to return to his family. Aurore had earnt £9 and twelve shillings during five years of service, but this was insufficient to pay her hospital expenses, and it was agreed to break her contract. It was decided that the unclaimed wages of those apprentices who died should be converted into a fund to pay the expenses of cases such as that of Aurore. When Frederick Lily Manya, apprenticed to a jeweller in the Chaussée, died in February 1847, however, very different plans had been laid for the disposal of the little income he possessed. The boy's wages altogether amounted to £30. The boy's first employer, a watchmaker, Mr Salusbury, had died earlier, and the jeweller to whom the boy had then been confided, claimed: 'knowing his intentions previous to his death, I am certain that what little he possessed ... he would have left it to his former mistress (the widow of Mr Salusbury) who when he was in her service took the greatest care of him, and whose circumstances at present are very distressing, having two young children to provide for'. The Procureur General, however, advised that the initial conditions of apprenticeship provided that any monies not paid over to the apprentices should 'be devoted to the purpose of forming a fund for rewarding good conduct or for the support of any of the individuals now to be apprenticed who may become unable to gain a livelihood'. Since Frederick had died without a will, his money had to be placed in the fund.[8]

Towards the close of 1843, the terms of apprenticeship of some 50 older Africans were due to expire. Acts of Freedom were drawn up for them and their wages withdrawn from the bank. They had received no monies at all during their term of service, and were thus presented with a lump sum. Those men who had served out two year indentures received a payment of £8 and eight shillings; women had earnt £4 and sixteen shillings over the same period. In the following year, when the four year apprenticeships likewise came to a close, the wages earnt by male Africans totalled £15 and twelve shillings, and that of females £7 and four shillings. Since these apprenticeships had begun, Indian immigration had reopened and wages had fallen dramatically. The African apprentices were thus advantaged by their fixed wage; they were not however happy at the arrangement which prevented them from receiving any portion of the money until the termination of their indentures. In July 1845 the Collector reported that 'much discontent is shown by the apprentices when they see their fellow servants receive their monthly wages and they receive nothing'. He accordingly arranged to pay out a portion of the money due to them in advance.[9]

In January 1846, a further 11 of the five year apprenticeships expired. Julien Lily Bombe was among those young men who collected £15 and 12 shillings due to him and Pauline Lily Pujean received £7 and four shillings. The youngest apprentices had two years left to complete, but employers now began to release them from their terms of service. In April 1846, the Tamil businessman, Tiroumoody, reported that his three apprentices, Mallac Lily Callumah, Antoine Lily Antou and Mazery Lily Masseah, 'have all been brought up to exercise some trade or pprofession by which they can earn a respectable livelihood, and that as their conduct ever since they entered his service has been irreproachable, he is willing to give up to them the remainder of the period of their apprenticeships'. The men were accordingly given their Acts of Freedom in May 1846. In November, Cunningham himself decided to release Victor Tiger Lily Mocjaw, his own apprentice, one year early:

> *I not only consider the individual referred to as perfectly able to earn a livelihood under a master of his own choosing but I am inclined to think that his age at the date of his indenture has been much underestimated and that instead of his being then only 9 years old, he cannot have been less than 11; he now appears to be at least 18 years old, at which age it was intended that all the individuals who when they were brought here were under 11 years of age should become their own masters.*

The names of the Africans clearly indicate that their original appellation was appended as a surname, that the ship which had rescued them was given to them as a middle name, and that when baptised they were given Christian first names. In Victor's case it is unclear whether his

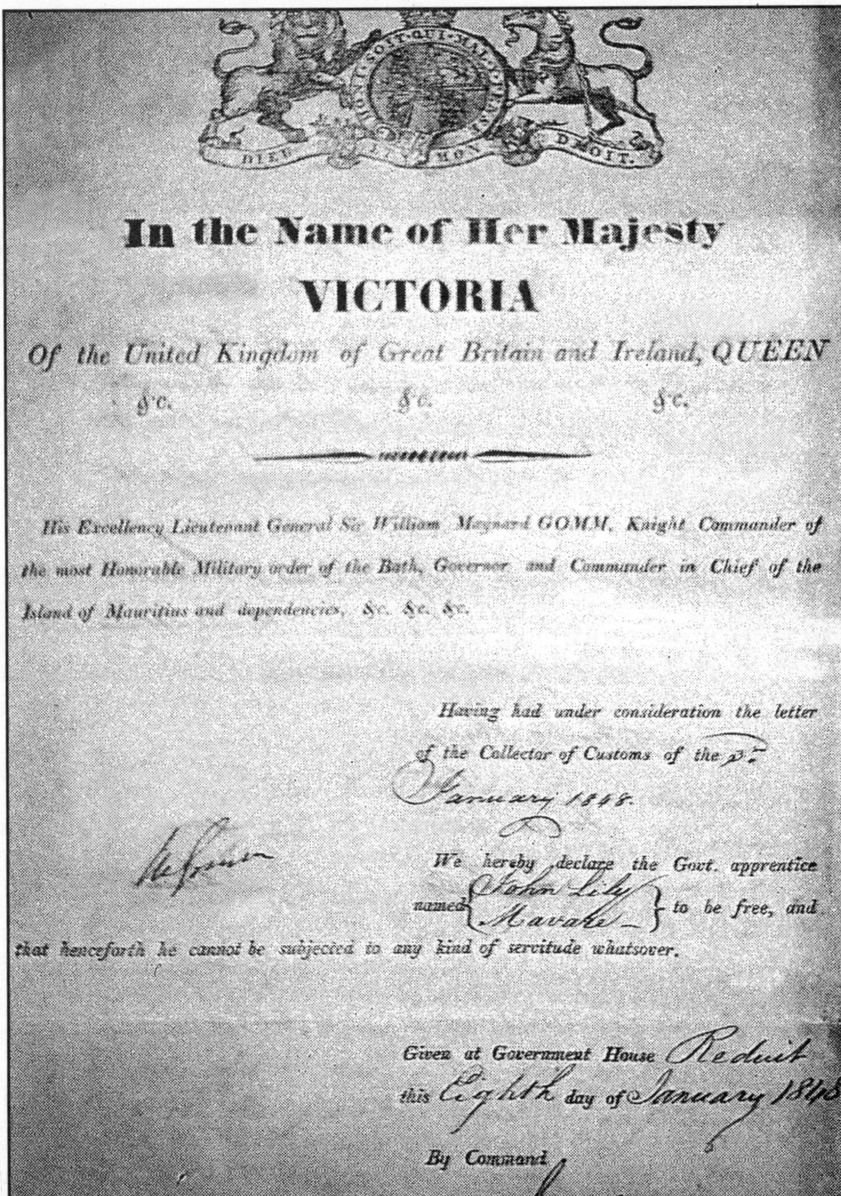

In the Name of Her Majesty

VICTORIA

Of the United Kingdom of Great Britain and Ireland, QUEEN

&c. &c. &c.

His Excellency Lieutenant General Sir William Maynard GOMM, Knight Commander of the most Honorable Military order of the Bath, Governor and Commander in Chief of the Island of Mauritius and dependencies, &c. &c. &c.

Having had under consideration the letter of the Collector of Customs of the 3d January 1848.

We hereby declare the Govt. apprentice named {John Lily Mavare} *to be free, and that henceforth he cannot be subjected to any kind of servitude whatsover.*

Given at Government House Reduit *this* Eighth *day of* January 1848.

By Command

The Act of Freedom of John Lily Mavare

transformation into 'Tiger Lily' was his own choice, or the result of another's fertile imagination![10]

If the conduct of most of the Africans had been pronounced irreproachable, this was not the case for Sambo Lily Combattoo and Hugon Lily. The former, a 21 year old domestic servant in the service of Major Cooper of the 35th Regiment, was accused in February 1846 of theft and given a three month prison sentence. At the trial it was reported that Sambo had

> *seul entrait dans la chambre à coucher de son maître, a profité du sommeil de celui-ci pour prendre la clef de son armoire qui se trouvait dans la poche de son pantalon pour ouvrir la dite armoire et enlever une bourse contenant dix sept piastres et quelques centimes.*

The purse was found in Sambo's room and he was duly convicted. Hugon Lily worked as a chauffeur for Mr Adrian of Plaines Wilhems. In February 1847, the 25 year old was accused of having 'volontairement porté de coups et blessures avec un bâton sur la personne du nommé Boncoeur Lily, se disant au service du Sieur Dick; et ce pendant que le dit Boncoeur Lily se trouvait dans sa case où il s'était rendu pour lui reclamer de l'argent qu'il lui devait'. However, the charge against him was not proven and he was exonerated.[11]

At the beginning of 1847, a number of women gained their Acts of Freedom, either because their periods of apprenticeship expired, or because, as in the cases of Anne Lily Yammoise and Matala Lily Mattiah, in the service of Mr Robinson and Mrs Sampson respectively, they were considered 'able to earn a livelihood' and desirous of obtaining their freedom. There was now a flood of letters indicating the employers' willingness to release their apprentices early. Lionel Lily Joacquin, still in England, was freed and presumably remained there, his wages of £15 and twelve shillings being sent on to him. Ned Lily Saddouma was freed in Mauritius by Mr Sanford; Thomas Hearn gave up the remainder of the apprenticeships of Paul Lily Monnalappa and Nancy Lily Cannemah in June, and Mr Richardson did the same for Pat Lily Pandou, now returned from India. In February 1848, Mary Lily Missaroah, the little girl who went to Australia with the Tapley family, was sent her wages and Act of Freedom in Adelaide, where she probably settled.[12]

During the remainder of 1848, the rest of the apprenticeships ended, and the claims for outstanding wages led to further information as to the whereabouts and behaviour of the Africans. Mollière, for example, informed the Governor that he had not seen Augustin Lily since October 1845 when that apprentice was transferred to his service by Mr George Coombes. Six days later, Augustin disappeared. The Collector of Customs likewise belatedly learned of the death of John Lily Mavure, apprenticed to Mr Milne, a baker, who had died in the Civil Hospital on 13 May 1847. Flore Lily Nammerson did not obtain her Act of Freedom until a year after it was due because she had absented herself in 1847 and was not found until February 1848. Three Africans were apprenticed to Mr Charreton, a planter in Flacq. One of them, Domingo Lily Domingo, was described as 'so very unsteady, so ill behaved and so frequently absent from his master's service that it became a question whether his indenture ought not to be broken and himself declared a maroon'. His wages were not paid for a year due to his frequent absences but then Domingo 'hearing that other of the Africans apprenticed at the same period with himself had got their money and Act of Freedom, has lately made frequent applications for his'. The Collector of Customs decided that Domingo was entitled to his outstanding wages but supported Charreton's statement that he should not be required to pay the last wage bill due because 'the boy did not serve him during any part of that year and was besides an utterly worthless character'.[13] The final settlement of accounts of the Africans whom Cunningham now referred to as the 'Lily Apprentices', was delayed by the failure of Mr R Duffau, an officer of the police stationed at Mahebourg, to pay the wages due to his apprentices, Charles Lily and Jeannette Lily, amounting in all to £13. The wages of Pat Lily Pandou conversely had to be paid back into the Treasury because he had absented himself from Richardson's service since April 1846 and not been heard of since.[14]

By mid 1848, then, the Collector's role as guardian of the young apprentices had ended. They had grown up in Mauritius and those that remained on the island were now free to work and live where they chose.

Julien Lily evidently took employ with the colonial administration as an interpreter for new immigrants arriving from Mozambique, for in 1861 he received two payments for his services when a number of liberated Africans disembarked in Mauritius from *HMS Sidon*.[15]

In the closing decades of the 19th century the by now aging Lily Africans began to reappear at the Customs and Immigration Departments requesting pensions and other financial assistance. In July 1879, Marie Thérèse Lily requested an increase to her pension. She had evidently married another Lily, as she was also described as Widow Dick Lily Quanasarah. The couple had settled in Moka, and become landowners, for she was described as

> *the owner of a plot of ground having one acre in extent in the vicinity of the sugar estate Hermitage ... she is 54 years old, and is in good health; she has with her 2 orphans, her grand-daughters, one 12 years old and the other 11 months; she receives monthly from Government 15 kilos of rice, 2 kilos of salt fish and 1 rupee, and every six months, the quantity of materials necessary to make up a suit of clothes.... The oldest girl would easily find an employer willing to give her food and clothing. If her grandmother prefers keeping her at home, it must be on condition of providing for her maintenance, which, after all, is a family duty incumbent upon her; and, moreover, the remuneration of the services very likely rendered to her by the girl.*

In November 1879, Mary Lily requested a pension in addition to that granted to her husband John Lily. They were another couple from amongst the Lily apprentices to have married. The Poor Law Commissioner reported on her case as follows:

> *her husband, John Lily, is in the receipt of rations and money from the Govt, and she asks for the same favor, because her fate and that of her aforenamed husband are identical: they were both rescued by the man-of-war Lily, brought to Mauritius and then engaged for fourteen years to Mr Saunders, who was then the owner of the sugar estate Bassin situated in the district of Plaines Wilhems; that after the expiry of that time they were liberated; that her husband, who is infirm, obtained rations*

from Government, but she had nothing; that she is now almost infirm, her sight being so impaired that she cannot do properly any work.... I have offered her to go and reside at Barkly Asylum; she has refused, alleging that she wishes to remain with her husband. Under these circumstances I can only suggest to give her, out of the Poor Law fund, fifteen kilos of rice per mensem and one rupee.[16]

Evidently, the word was spreading amongst the Africans that the Government was prepared to accord them pensions in the form of rations, for in the same month Cubitt Lily Mattiah also applied for aid. However, in this case, the Commissioner, Ducray, declared that the 55 year old man was 'well able to work and earn a livelihood, and is not entitled to assistance'. Cubitt, like Mary, refused an offer from Ducray to be employed on light gardening jobs at the Barkly Asylum. The aging Mozambicans valued their independence.[17]

More of the Lily apprentices applied for government pensions around the turn of the century. Zepha Lily Ejaffah, who lived at Phoenix on the premises of Mr Badal, near the Police Station, appeared at the Immigration Department in January 1896. She was nearly blind. By this stage, the Government was no longer aware of the circumstances in which the Lilys had arrived in Mauritius. Zepha Lily helpfully offered to elucidate her origins by promising to 'bring a ticket of one of her friends who receives pension, and who came on the same ship with her'. From their own enquiries the Store Keeper General's office ascertained that some Africans were designated as 'Government Emancipated Invalids'. The criteria were that the individuals had to have been 'liberated from some slaver and taken on as an apprentice by government'. In their ignorance, the officials decided that Zepha Lily 'does not come under this designation'. Because she was 70 years of age and with weak eyesight, the Poor Law Commission was disposed to offer her admission into the Barkly Asylum. Eventually, in May 1896, Zepha Lily was able to produce her act of freedom, given to her in 1846 and thereby establish her right to maintenance.[18]

Some of the Lily apprentices married into the Creole and Indian communities. In 1847, Mr B Labutte, the employer of Marianne Lily

Marianne agreed to 'renounce the year of her apprenticeship which has to run, in consequence of the application of her husband Carime Bacosse that she may receive her freedom from indenture and be enabled to reside with him'. It was perhaps not so surprising that a baptised apprentice should marry a Muslim given that numbers of the Mozambicans had surnames which suggested a link to that faith, as in the case of Clare Lily Dinamacou.[19] A Louise Ticklan who married a Lily, died in 1870, a Mlle Cadinet is also registered as having done so, before her death in 1880. In 1875 Auguste Joseph Lily Laharko married Marie Rose Bellepeau in Port Louis. Marie Pauline Peromez entered into a union with a member of the Lily community when she wed Pierre Ostrange Lily at Plaines Wilhems in 1877, and a female Lily, Amélie Nanseehah, married Eugène Louis Pirally of Black River in 1880. As we have seen some Lilys married other Lilys: in 1867 the death of Mrs Lily, née Lily, was recorded.[20]

The civil status registers which record the births, deaths and marriages of the Lily Africans also offer a demonstration of the gradual disappearance of the African surnames of the Lilys. Already between 1860 and 1870, most of the Lilys who die are not recorded as having an African name. However, Julius Maussino Lily, born in 1876 at Pamplemousses, conserved his as a middle name. Sadly, it was only for the benefit of the register which bears his name; he died the same day. Louise Marie Lily Matalah conserved her African name until her death in 1884. A man recorded as Lily Mattiah, probably Cubitt, died in 1900. By the 1880s onwards, most of the Lilys who marry and are born in Mauritius have no other names. Marie Lily married a Tamil, Mooniapa Tirvetty, in Plaines Wilhems in 1882; Rose Lily married Jean Baptiste Songor at Moka in 1888 and Lala Lily married a man named Louis Ferdinand Bothanaire in 1890. The final appearance of a Lily with an African name in the civil status registers is that of James Moussina Lily, who died at Pamplemousses in 1920.[21]

It was perhaps not surprising that the African heritage of the Lily apprentice so quickly disappeared from view. Most of those who arrived were children; their indentures bound their employers to instruct the apprentices in the principles of Christian worship and to baptise them within two years. Some of the women entered into relationships with Asian men, but most merged into the Creole community.

An Unbroken Link: Koomanikooa and his Descendants

Retracing the paths of African immigrants in Mauritius and discovering their lineages is a difficult process because so many African names have failed to survive the passage of time. With some persistence, however, it is possible to follow the story of an individual African settler through the diverse historical records available in Mauritius. The story of Koomanikooa is one such - a simple and precise link between the Creole present and the African past.

Koomanikooa arrived in Mauritius in July 1868. He was one of 7 men, 3 women and 8 children who disembarked from the *Admiral*. They were all 'Liberated Africans', or individuals sold and shipped as slaves and who were intercepted by British cruizers and taken to safe ports. Once in Mauritius or elsewhere, they were allotted to local employers for a specified contractual period and these contracts were completed, they were considered free immigrants. Koomanikooa was 14 years old at the time of his arrival. He was just over 5 feet tall and had a round scar on his forehead. He was entrusted to the employ of one V. Dupont in Port Louis on 20 July 1868 for a period of five years. Koomanikooa was listed as No 4. His second name - supposedly his mother's name - was given as Ayoyelamah. In 1874, Koomanikooa, then aged around 20, applied for and was granted, on 3rd July, a Certificate of Non Marriage. This was designed to enable him to declare himself single and to contract marriage. So Koomanikooa had evidently found himself a female partner. But it was not until 1883 that he finally tied the knot. His wife was Eleonore Smarle, presumably a Christian Creole woman. They married at Plaines Wilhems on 21st July of that year.[22] Interestingly, Koomanikooa's name had already undergone a distortion. His mother's name - with the spelling slightly altered - was now listed as his first name, and that of Koomanikooa had metamorphosed into his family name. It was thus that Avryslamah Koomanikooa (4) entered the annals of the colony, the founding father of a family dynasty which is still present in Mauritius today.

Les faits qui ont valu au constable Koomanikooa la "George Medal"

In 1873 a child, Julia, was born. Jeanne Koomanikooa was the second daughter, born in 1785. Three more children were born between 1883 and 1889, including a son, Joseph Emmanuel Koomani Kooa. More male Koomanikooas were born in the 1890s, so that by the turn of the century, Koomanikooa's male offspring were able to carry on his name. The family flourished, as the career of Hervé Koomanikooa, born in 1926 in Curepipe, would show.[23] He became a policeman, and his daring interception of a notorious criminal made the headlines in 1960, leading to the conferring of the George Medal on Hervé in 1961. *Le Mauricien* carried the story on the front page of its edition of 28 April 1961, describing how the valiant officer had given chase to Menville Villard, braving several shots fired in his direction, and a struggle during which Villard produced a knife and narrowly missed stabbing him, ripping his trousers. The newspaper ended its account of Hervé's story with the information: 'Hervé Koomanikooa est le petit fils d'un Africain qui était venu s'établir à Maurice'. Today the Lily and Koomanikooa family names are often seen in the newspapers, as the descendants of Mozambican immigrants continue to make their presence felt in Mauritius through sporting and other feats.

This article has demonstrated that the search for African roots is not beyond the reach of Afro-Creoles in quest for information about their past. There are no doubt many other African family names which can yield up their history with a small amount of effort. At the same time, the story of the Lily apprentices highlights the ways in which unfamiliar African names become lost, particularly where immigrants arrive as children, spend their formative years in the care of other communities, and adopt new names. Finally, this paper has sought to dispel the notion that Afro-Mauritian history is lost in the mists of the past - the continuing arrival of African immigrants up to the last quarter of the 19th century is ample proof of the availability of a written record of the presence and contribution of immigrants from that continent.

References

1. MA RA 18 Collector of Customs to Colonial Secretary, 4 Oct 1816 and see Lubbock, 1955: 24.
2. MA SA 30 Lord Russell to Governor of Mauritius, 20 April 1840.
3. MA SD 19 Smith to Russell, 6, 13 Aug 1840.
4. MA RA 603 Collector of Customs to Colonial Secretary, 29 June, 31 Aug, 24 Nov 1840.
5. MA RA 652 Collector to Colonial Secretary 12 Feb, 2 March 1841.
6. MA SD 19 Smith to Russell 22 May 1841 (44); RA 700 C Trevelyan, Treasury, to Commissioners Customs, 15 March 1842.
7. RA 700 Cunningham to Col Secy 19 June 1842, Encl: James Wilson to Cunningham, Champ de Mars, 17 Jan 1842; Cunningham to Col Secy 4 April 1842; R Tapley to E Cardew, 7 Nov1842; RA 814 Collector to Col Secy 13 March 1845; RA 859 Collector to Col Secy, 18 Feb 1846.
8. MA RA 814 Ducray to Collector 10 Nov 1845; RA 859 Collector of Customs to Col Secy 21Jan 1846; RA 908 Collector of Customs, 3 March 1847; Eug`ne Leigauye to Cunningham, 24 March 1847; Report of d'Epinay, 31 May 1847.
9. MA RA 745 Collector of Customs to Colonial Secretary 28 Sept, 28 Oct, 28 Nov 1843; RA 775 20 Dec 1844; RA 814 Collector of Customs to Col Secy 18 July 1845.

10. MA RA 859 Collector of Customs to Col Secy 13 Jan , 29 Apr, 9 May, 5 Nov 1846.

11. MA JA 86 27 Feb 1846; JA 89 12 Feb 1847.

12. MA RA 908 Collector of Customs to Col Secy 19 Feb, 2, 17 March, 1, 17 April, 14 June, 9 Oct 1847; RA 966 16 Feb 1848.

13. MA RA 985 JT Mollière Petition to Governor, 29 March 1847; RA 966 Collector of Customs to Col Secy 3 Feb, 12, 22 Feb, 5 March 1848.

14. MA RA 966 22 March, 5 June 1848.

15. PRO CO 167/438 Appendix K, Charles Wing, Collector of Customs, March and May 1861.

16. MA Z4B Vol 7 Ducray Report no 226, 17 July of 17.7.79; L.R. No 6480, Ducray Report No 312, 4 Nov 1879

17. MA Z4B L.R. No 6482 Cubit Lily Mattiah 6 Nov 1879.

18. MGI PL 9 Col. Secy to Protector 24 Jan 1896, Mins, May 1896.

19. MA RA 908 Collector of Customs to Col Secy 19 Feb 1847; RA 859 Jan 1846.

20. MA KL 18 - Table of Marriages, 1871 to 1880; KL 7 - Table of Deaths, 1861 to 1870.

21. MA KL 12 - Births, from 1871 to 1880; KL 28 Tables of Marriages from 1881 to 1890; KL 31 Tables of Births from 1891 to 1900; KL 36 Tables of Deaths from 1891 to 1900; KL 63 Tables of Deaths for 1911 to 1920

22. MA KL 27 Tables of Marriages from 1881 to 1890.

23. Koomanikooa entries in MA KL 12, KL 20, KL 31, 36 and 73.

Cavadee and Kalimai: Inter-Ethnic Participation in Mauritian Rituals

Pavi Ramhota[1] *and Vishwanaden Govinden*[2]

This article looks at two religious rituals currently practised in Mauritius and assesses the processes of adaptation and transformation they have undergone in the context of the pluri-ethnic society within which they co-exist. Firstly, this study deals with a magico-religious ritual called *'Baharia Puja'* associated with fertility, with the protection of the village and its inhabitants from evil spirits, and with attempts to ensure a good harvest. This ritual is performed by the bhojpuri-speaking Hindus whose ancestors came from North India as indentured labourers to Mauritius during the period 1834-1910. Baharia Puja takes place in the shrines dedicated to the goddess Kali at the place of worship called *kalimai*. Kalimai, the religious site where rituals and prayers are performed, is usually located in an open space outside the village or at its boundary. The shrine consists of an altar on which seven heads made of stones are placed - representing the seven sisters in popular Hinduism. The goddess Mother Kali is the main deity. The altar may alternatively be housed in a small concrete building. Outside the shrine, there are several male deities who exercise different functions in the ritualistic system. *Cavadee* is a Tamil religious festival celebrated in the months of January and February (*Thaipoosum Cavadee*) corresponding with the Tamil month 'Thai', and in April-May (*Sittirai Cavadee*). The festival is dedicated to Lord Muruga. Participation in Cavadee involves a personal sacrifice which often begins with a prayer that has been fulfilled. The individual who has been thus blessed decides to offer his tribute to God at Cavadee. Participants may decide to perform a number of penances such as walking barefoot on nails, piercing the tongue and cheeks and so on. Prior to the festival itself, devotees must fast for a period of 10 days, a period defined by the raising of a flag called *kodiyetum*. During this time, prayers and devotional songs are sung at Tamil temples. Fire walking is a ritual associated with Cavadee, and is a penance performed for the Goddess Ammen. Fire walking is also sometimes performed by Tamils within the premises of the kalimai. Kalimai rituals, based around simple structures and located on plantations, are probably among the earliest forms of worship practised by indentured labourers. The practice of Cavadee in Mauritius dates at least as far back as the early 19th century when it was a festival in which all Hindus participated. The continuing importance of these festivals today enables us to appreciate the continuity of forms of popular Hinduism in the overseas context.

Indian Settlement in Mauritius

Sugar cane was first introduced by the Dutch, but Mauritius remained a predominately commerce-based economy until 1825 when the British equalised sugar duties in an effort to build up the economy based upon large scale sugar production in plantations (Deerr, 1942). The expansion of the sugar industry coincided with emancipation and the end of slavery. The planters drew upon previous experience of Indian labour (principally Tamil in the French period) to introduce indentured workers from the subcontinent (Carter, 1995). During 1834-1910 as many as 450,000 Indians arrived in the island, although around one third of them went back to India after only a few years, when their contracts expired (North Coombes, 1990). The island of Mauritius now has a population of approximately 1.2 million. The majority consists of the Hindu population with 51% but it is subdivided into several distinct linguistic categories. The Bhojpuri speaking Hindus, according to the 1983 census, comprise 40% of the population of Mauritius. The Tamils who came from Southern India are the second largest ethnic group (13.9%), followed by the Telegus (5.6%) and the Marathis (4%). Today, despite the adherence of all four ethnic groups to the Hindu religion, the term 'hindou' or 'indien' in Mauritius is now exclusively identified with the Bhojpuri majority.

The planters (mostly of White, European origin) and the indentured labourers (introduced mainly from Eastern and Southern India), were thrown together in a single pursuit - the production of sugar cane. In the Mauritian context, this meant living in estate camps on sugar plantations in large population units. Plantations were fully integrated into the economic and social order of Mauritius, and as a result, land became important in social relationships and social organisation. The Whites had their own emotional attachment to the plantations - where the old buildings were named after their ancestors. At first, there were no temples for the Hindus to practise their religion. From the mid 19th century the White planters bequeathed small portions of land approximately 30 ft by 30 ft to associations of their workers to build religious shrines and altars. The kalimai became one such religious site which was erected in the sugar cane plantations. Later, amassing funds from within their own communities to build more grandiose structures, the *kovil*, the *mandir* and the mosque became an established feature of the Mauritian landscape.

Whilst the sacred topography of Hindus in Mauritius was under construction, Hindus continued to join in festivals such as Yamsé, (also known as ghoun, Tazzia or Muharram) which while Shia Muslim in origin, was an inter-religious event in South India, from which region it probably came to Mauritius in the 18th century. In the early 19th century, it continued to be a major festival for Hindus and Sunni Muslims alike, as sugar estate workers were given leave only at New Year, two days for Muharram, and one day to attend the races, as annual holidays (Carter, 1995: 262). Nicholas Pike, U.S. Consul in Mauritius in the mid 19th century, reported that on some of the sugar estates it was a major festival with the ghouns 'being subscribed for by all the Indians in the camp; and they get leave from their masters to go round to the various private houses in the vicinity to display them'. Pike attended a Yamsé procession in Port Louis where he noted that some of the ghouns were 'carried on the heads of negroes hired for the purpose, not Mahommedans' (Pike, 1873: 138-9). Other contemporary accounts of Yamsé depict the cosmopolitan character of the crowd who attended (*Progrès Colonial*, 3 April 1871).

Although on one level the colonial administration denounced the 'heathenism' of Indians and denigrated their cultural practices, at another level practical concessions to incorporate Hindu and Muslim religious needs within the plantation routine were made by individual planters. There thus existed a relatively cordial interaction between the Whites and indentured labourers at work, although they remained separate from each other after work. The villagers called those Whites *saheb* or *kaptan.* Despite being the bearers of very different cultural traditions, the kaptans and the Indians co-inhabited the estate, where a limited cultural intercourse took place.

Unlike most other indentured-labour importing territories, in Mauritius ownership of cane lands passed very rapidly into the hands of the Indians by the end of the 19th century. There were a number of reasons for this. One was economic: a combination of natural calamities and low sugar prices in the last 19th century had an adverse impact on the entire economy of the country, and the Whites abandoned cultivation to concentrate their economic role in sugar processing. This led to the *grand morcellement* in the 1880's whereby Indians bought plots of land to become smallholders of sugar plantations. Secondly, immigrant Indians were believed in Mauritius to be a replacement labour force, and ex-slaves were incorporated less and less into the mainstream economy. As a result, from the mid 19th century, the large scale settlement of families and kin groups was encouraged by the colonial state (Allen, 1983). The fortunate few became landowners, and used their economic power to become cultural benefactors.

Those Hindus and Muslims who started their own cultivation of sugar cane naturally encountered the same economic difficulties faced by White planters, and their rituals and religious ceremonies were often employed to alleviate the sufferings associated with poverty, and cyclical disasters. When the plantations were affected by natural calamities which reduced the production of sugar cane, the Indians turned to magico-religious rituals which were often performed at the kalimai shrine. This offered them hope for a reversal of fortunes or some solace at times of anxiety.

The Nature and Calendar of Hindu Rituals in Mauritius

As the Hindu communities began settling in the island, new types of collectively structured socio-religious phenomena developed. From the second half of the 19th century North Indian Hindus began to make an annual pilgrimage to Grand-Bassin (now a sacred lake and Hindu place of worship) which is located in the south of the island. This pilgrimage continues to take place each March and is celebrated as Maha Shivratri. It attracts devotees from all over the island and even abroad, for example many South African Hindus attend. Hindus from other linguistic categories also participate. Tamil and Marathi speaking Hindus attend prayers held at Grand Bassin. Shivatri has thus become, in Mauritius, a pan-Hindu and a public festival. The Shivratri festival is one of the most popular Hindu celebrations. The devotees of Shiva go to the sacred lake on foot and keep vigil the whole night, singing devotional songs, offering sweetmeats to Lord Shiva and eating the *prasad* (blessed food) as they have to stay for two days. Water from the sacred lake is carried back to the respective temples where the devotees pour it on the aniconic linga of Shiva - the phallic representation of Shiva. In Mauritius there are numerous temples known as “Shiv Mandir” and Lord Shiva has a large number of devotees.

In the month of February-March the festival of Holi (Pagwa) is celebrated among the Northern Hindus. During this celebration the Hindus dance, sing *chowtal* (devotional songs) and play with red colours (*abir*). The Navratri festival, or 'the nine nights', is celebrated twice a year in Mauritius, in April and October. It is dedicated to Mother Durga with the singing of *bhajans*, (devotional songs) and recital of hymns from the sacred scriptures of Hinduism. This festival commemorates the victory of the goddess Durga over the demon king Mahishasura who by his boon granted by Brahma defeated and dominated the gods. The goddess Durga severed his buffalo-head. The Durga Puja is the only *puja* for which Sanatanist Hindus throughout the country observe strict fasts.

The Diwali *(parab)* festival, of lights is also held in October. According to the epic of Ramayana, the return of Ram to Ayodhya (the birth place of Ram) after a long period of 14 years of exile in the forest, is celebrated. Hindus of all linguistic groups light small, coconut oil-fuelled *diya* (earthen lamps) in front of their houses and yards. Sweets are made and exchanged between coreligionists and distributed to neighbours and friends of other ethnic groups. Divali has become in Mauritius, like Eid, an occasion when one ethnic group has an opportunity to invite others to share in their festivities. In addition Diwali is today celebrated with lavish open-air cultural shows which all Mauritians and visitors are encouraged to attend.

The Practice of Kalimai

Both in the rural and urban areas the kalimai cults form an integral system of communication and exchange which has been deeply rooted in the plantation society, and represent early forms of social integration for the indentured labourers. Those descendants of Hindu immigrants who identify themselves with *Sanatanist* (orthodox hindu) practices are more consistent users of the kalimai than the adherents of the *Arya Samaj* (a reform movement). The various uses to which the kalimai are put, are also defined by the caste of worshippers. Thus the Sudras, the lower castes, used the kalimai to perform animal sacrifice. Members of the Brahminical caste prefer offering certain vegetables or fruits to the deity. The goddess Kali is mostly prayed to by women, whereas men generally perform the animal sacrifices. Alcohol and non-vegetarian foods are also offered to the protective deity of the village who is called *Dhi* in Bhojpuri, and known by the term *ministre prince* in Creole. In this way, the plantation and village as social and territorial units obtained protection against the works of evil spirits.

The abode of the Dhi or protector of the village is situated under a tree because at night he is believed to come out and rest there. The Dhi makes nocturnal visits to every nook and cranny of the village making sure that there is no evil haunting the place. Some villagers leave a recipient of water uncovered in their houses so that the Dhi could quench his thirst. The Dhi is prayed to at intervals varying between montly and annual worship. The Dhi is believed to favour offerings such as candles, sardines, bread, cigarettes and rum. This deity is worshipped by most villagers in Mauritius irrespective of ethnic group, because as protector of the village, he matters to everyone.

In some Mauritian villages, the Dhi, who also symbolises a non-hindu spirit, is believed to reside in the kalimai. The Dhi is worshipped first before entering the kalimai and the worshippers have to ask him for permission to go inside the premises. The Dhi is supposed to have been there even before the construction of the kalimai just as the Whites were already in Mauritius when the Indians arrived. In the Mauritian context, the Dhi can therefore be associated with the White planter. He is called *grand dimoune* which is a term the Indians used for those Whites who donated them lands to cultivate some vegetables on or to grow grass for their cattle.

Those who fail to respect the deity are believed to suffer the consequences. It is reported that after the *grand morcellement* at the end of the 19th century those Indians who purchased plots of sugar cane land, and in so doing tried to uproot the abode of Dhi, experienced great loss or even faced death. The Whites also were reluctant to interfere with the kalimai or to fell trees found in the shrine for fear that some misfortune might happen to them. One informant from the village of Clemencia (situated in the eastern part of the island with about 2,500 inhabitants) described how a *saheb* who was the proprietor of a sugar factory went for a ride in his horse drawn carriage or *carriole* and met with a fatal accident. During those days there was no specific place or part of the land set aside as a cremation or burial ground. The saheb was therefore buried on his own land as were other family members. People lit candles and made offerings to them and this became a tradition for the villagers. Hence, an established relationship has developed between the Dhi and the kalimai as between the Whites and the Indians, for the Whites were also seen as the provider of their livelihoods and their protectors.

The kalimai is not only a place where deities are worshipped but also the abode of the *dayn*, witches who practice their "profession" to bring harm to the people of the village by their evil spells. At the village of Clemencia a group of five elderly female informants described how, before the building of the local kalimai in concrete, there were only seven trees planted by their ancestors located on the estate. The seven women immigrants of the village assembled there and practised their black magic far into the night. Later on, this place was converted into a kalimai called Petit Verger. This kalimai is considered to be more powerful than the other kalimai. It has become a great place of worship for both the labourers and the planters. The practice of black magic in Mauritius extends to all communities. Sorcerors or *longanistes* practice their art at sites believed to propitious such as cemeteries or crossroads. In this way Christian sites are visited by Hindus and Muslims for the purpose of making sacrifices and conducting spells. At times of crisis, superstitions can take on a national dimension. The widespread fear of the *loupgarou* (werewolf) in Mauritius after the devastation of cyclone Hollanda in 1994 is a case in point.

At kalimai, as elsewhere, then, rituals act as an integrative force between supernatural forces and human beings. In the past, before the harvest of sugar cane, a Baharia Puja was performed. Each sugar factory began its harvest at a particular time, and before harvesting, the White planters in F.U.E.L.(Flacq United Estates Limited which is the biggest sugar factory in the island), offered financial assistance to the Indian labourers to perform the animal sacrifice so as to make the harvest prosperous. Religious spending was a highly profitable investment for the future and a source of prestige and pleasure in the present. Nowadays, financial aid to perform rituals is no longer allocated to the practitioners or users of the kalimai by the White estate owner. Gradually the kalimai are being converted into small temples and run by local Hindu associations. However gifts to people and to the Gods have both served the purpose of bringing peace between them. In this way evil spirits and, more generally, bad influences, are got rid of. The estate owner in Mauritius is perceived by the Indians as giving *dan* (gift) whilst the Indians in turn perform *balidan* (sacrifice) in order to bring prosperity to the village. Dan is linked to wealth accumulation whilst balidan is seen as an instrument of welfare. The balidan sacrifice of goats, also called 'kansi puja', is carried out in the rural areas in the premises of the kalimai. This cult is performed only by North Indians in Mauritius whereas in the Caribbean the *puja* of kalimai is carried out by the South Indian Tamils. (Vertovec, 1992;

Phillips, 1960; Khan, 1977; Bassier, 1987). In Mauritius, this puja is not carried out only for the Hindu community, but for all the communities living in the village and its welfare, for the health of the children and also for the protection of the village from all types of calamities, diseases, and evils.

In some quarters of the island, Tamils and North Indian Hindus practise fire walking in the premises of the kalimai together, for example at St Julien d'Hotman, Beau Vallon and even at Cassis kalimai. Fire walking and walking on swords were formerly quite common at Cassis kalimai, but the practise has now ceased. Recourse to the kalimai by Tamils was in part a reaction to disputes between Tamil associations at the various kovils. In present day Mauritius, Tamils have recourse to kalimai to pray if these are conveniently located. Tamil priests and healers may perform prayers at kalimai.

The Practice of Cavadee

When the Tamils arrived in Mauritius, they brought with them not only their labour and their skills, but also their religious beliefs. The importance of the cultural traditions which they sought to adapt to their new setting has been underscored by a historian of the indenture system:

> *The only occasions on which the estate Indians emerged from their condition of servitude to create some replication of the colour and majesty of their native land was during the time of festivals. Even amid the harsh conditions of plantation life, they were allowed to commemorate their ancient traditions and in time the Indian festivals became an integral part of the seasonal cycle of all the sugar islands.* (Tinker, 1974: 215)

The first Tamil temple to be constructed in Mauritius, by Sinnatambou, was at Terre Rouge, and was consecrated in 1846 (Sooriamoorthy, 113-40). Another group of Tamils in Mauritius purchased a plot of land on which to site a second temple in 1854. The plot of 10 acres and 30 perches at Rivière des Lataniers, had been acquired from Emilien de Boucherville and the price raised by a subscription. The intention was to construct 'a Hindoo chapel under the denomination of 'Sokalingum Minatchy Ammene', and also for building a free school for teaching the Tamil language'. The solidarity of Tamils throughout the island for the project was evinced by the main motive of the petition:

A depiction of Cavadee in late 19th Century Mauritius, showing spectators of many ethnic groups.

That for the maintenance of the said chapel and school, the undersigned are desirous of forming a voluntary subscription among all classes of their sect, and the labouring population having evinced a desire to contribute, it is necessary to send two emissaries, men of trust, but of the old immigration, to visit the different districts of the island ....

That the beneficial result to immigration arising from these salutary measures ... But now the ritual of his religion being observed in the island, that incentive to leave will be removed, and in lieu of a passing resident, the Hindoo will gradually become a permanent denizen of the land.

It seemed to be the intention of the petitioners to conduct their procession within the grounds of the land itself, and distinguished in this respect their festival from existing rites then celebrated in Mauritius: 'the annual fete ... similar in some respects to the usual Indian festival, differs in this point that the enceinte of the House of Worship is selected for the holy procession'. [3]

In 1868, Nicholas Pike visited the Tamil temple at Terre Rouge, managed by Sinnatambou, where he witnessed Cavadee ceremonies for which 'Crowds gathered from all parts of the island. Every railway train was full to overflowing'. At Roche Bois he saw a Timithi ceremony:

Piles of wood were burning, which in about an hour became a bed of live embers. Two nude men, having long-handled rakes, were employed in getting out the unburnt pieces of wood, and distributing the embers over a square of about 25 feet ... Everything being pronounced ready by the priest who superintended the whole, music was heard in the distance, and a procession moved along the grassy plain, preceded by men bearing on their shoulders a small platform, on which was an image dressed in Indian costume, loaded with jewellery. They came on in silence and halted near the burning mass. Presently another similar procession advanced from the opposite side, and faced the first. At a given signal, an old man, with only a cloth round his loins, bearing a child in his arms, stepped into the square, and walked unflinchingly across the glowing bed of embers.

In present day Mauritius, the celebration of Thaipoosum Cavadee is considered by Tamils to be the most important of the rituals they undertake, and has been accorded a public holiday by the Government. There are several other religious occasions called Cavadee which are celebrated by Mauritian Tamils at different times of the year, but Thaipoosum in January-February and Sittirai in April-May are the most significant.

The word Cavadee is derived from the Tamil for *kaavu* (to carry) and *thadi* (polished wood), and refers to the structures carried by devotees during the ceremonies. According to popular legend, the sage Agastiya requested his most devoted disciple Idumban to bring for him the two mountain peaks of 'Sivagari' and 'Saktigiri' donated to him by *Shiva.* When Idumban reached Mount Kailasum (Shiva's abode), he removed the two peaks, tied them to a pole, and placing the pole on his shoulders, started his journey back to Agastiya. It is said that on his way he stopped to rest. At this point *Muruga*, the second son of Shiva, took the form of a small boy, and stood on one of the peaks, so that Idumban could not lift his burden. He then noticed the boy and a fight broke out between them but Idumban was defeated by Muruga. From then on, he became a servant of Muruga, and is always found standing by his side.

Cavadee, which represents an obeisance to Lord Muruga, re-enacts this journey in that devotees carry their offerings to the deity supported on their shoulders. Muruga is himself one of the most ancient deities worshipped by Tamils. He is known by different appellations such as Arumugam, who rides on a peacock, has six heads and brandishes numerous weapons in his 12 hands; and also as Subramanian, meaning a person who attends to the spiritual growth of aspirants; and as *Kartigeya*, who is reputedly born to and reared by the six divine mothers of the constellation Krttika. Kartigeya is also known as the God of War. Finally, Muruga is also known as Velayuden, who is represented as *vel*, the spear that dispels the darkness of ignorance and evil. Muruga is a substitute for the glory and power of Shiva and finds a place in Shaivism.

The rite of Cavadee begins 10 days before the festival itself, with the commencement of a period of fasting. The date on which this begins is regulated by the Tamil calendar which is consulted by the officiating priest of each participating temple. The beginning of the fast is announced by the raising of a temple flag, the *kodiyetum.* Devotees from this time until the Cavadee consume only vegetarian food, practice sexual abstinence, and may sleep on a mat on the floor. During this period they attend the temple regularly to participate in prayer and devotional songs. On the morning that

Cavadee takes place, devotees make *archanai* and *paal abhishekam*, ie offerings of coconuts, milk and fruits to Muruga. A purificatory bath is taken on the banks of a river which is accompanied by prayers, before the procession itself starts. Some devotees are pierced with needles in elaborate patterns with interlinking chains, others with hooks from which limes are suspended. The piercing used to be carried out by jewellers; nowadays it is undertaken by anyone with the requisite training. This ritual is part of the sacrifice offered by devotees. The adepts walk with their Cavadees in procession from the river bank to the temple. On the Cavadees are attached two brass pots known as *sombu.* These contain offerings for Muruga. On arrival at the temple, participants hand the pots to the priest who offers the milk contained in them to the deity. Once this is completed, the fast can be broken, and devotees are offered food. The practice of feeding participants is, in itself considered a worthy act, known as *annadanam.*

Another form of Cavadee which is practised in Mauritius and which is dedicated to the goddesses Draupadi, Mariamman, Karumari and Kaliamman, is Timithi, or the fire walking ceremony. This is generally celebrated around December and January, and exceptionally in March. Timithi begins with the same observances as described above. In addition, during the fasting period, an *ekium*, or purification ceremony, is performed at the *kuzhi*, or pit where the coals will be placed. On the day of Timithi itself, devotees make offerings of honey, sugar, coconut water, curd, milk, turmeric water and *panchamudam* (mixed fruits) to the deities. A *kankanam* (turmeric wrapped inside a thread) is tied to the hands of those participating, the purpose of which is to protect the devotee from evil. At the river bank, *karakam*, (a brass pot decorated with flowers and neem leaves, containing turmeric water) is prepared along with *agni chatti* (a container with a flame), these will be carried to the temple. On arrival at the temple, the devotee carrying the karakam is the first to walk across the *kuzhi* in which hot coals have been placed. Male devotees then walk through the pit, followed by women and children. Once Timithi is completed, the fast is broken, and on the next day the *kodi irakkam* takes place, or the taking down of the flag.

Cavadee has become an event of significance not only to Tamils, but to other ethnic groups. It is now common to see Mauritians of many different faiths making vows to participate in this ritual. According to the officiating priest of a participating temple, amongst devotees at the 1997 celebration of Cavadee at the Mariammen temple of Port Louis, were Hindus of Telegu and

Marathi speaking groups.[4] The interviewee had witnessed Chinese participants at past Cavadee festivals, and mentioned that Christians regularly took part. Such individuals generally came of their own accord to the priest prior to the celebration of Cavadee to enquire about the preparations to be made for participation. Such individuals perform all aspects of Cavadee along with the Tamil devotees: fasting, ritual purifications, piercing of the body and participation in fire walking. Some Christian participants continued to attend Church at the same time as fasting for Cavadee, so that taking part in the Tamil Hindu rite is not seen as affecting their continuing adherence to their Christian observances. However, it was recorded by the interviewee that some Christian participants also kept a shrine to Muruga at their homes, suggesting a more tangible and permanent attachment to Hindu practices. The proximity to and belief in the efficacity of Cavadee have evidently led to some syncretic religious observances in modern Mauritius. The priest also noted the indirect participation of Muslims in Cavadee through donations made to the temple and through offerings presented to the priest. Individuals of other ethnic groups co-operated in the festival of Cavadee in other ways. The procession to the Mariammen temple of Port Louis passes through Plaine Verte. Muslim residents assist the devotees by providing water to cool the streets along which the barefoot participants walk. Most of the Cavadee festivals celebrated in Mauritius attract an audience, en route and at the temple, of tourists and Mauritians of all ethnic groups. Tamils from Reunion, Seychelles and South Africa are also known to participate in Cavadee and to make the journey specifically to Mauritius for this purpose.

Kalimai worship demonstrates the cross-cultural importance of supernatural beliefs and the incorporation of existing social realities into ritual. Thus the pre-eminence of the persons of the White planter and their families in the lives of Indian labourers was translated into their worship as *grand dimounes*, *Kaptans* or *sahebs* at popular places of worship. For their part, the estate owners collaborated in the implementation of these religious sites through donations of land and money. The power relationships integral to the plantation and later the estate village are reflected in these forms of prestation and worship. As Foucault has argued, power is everywhere, it is not an entity or a commodity that can be possessed or given. In praying to the Kaptan, the Indians have both acknowledged the power inherent in their social relationship with Whites but have also harnessed that power to their own ends. In the same way, in multi-cultural Mauritius the power which is believed to be vested in the deities of individual ethnic groups can be shared and disseminated to other communities through their participation in ritual and festival. The simple act of setting off fire crackers to ward off evil spirits as practised by the Chinese has thus been adopted across the ethnic spectrum as a simple and effective means of protecting places of abode or business and as an expression of general celebration. In the same way Cavadee has become a significant festival not only to Tamils in Mauritius but to participants of other ethnic groups who have been inspired by the manifestation of faith of devotees willing to pierce their bodies and to walk on hot coals. Christians and others have been inspired by this demonstration of the power of Muruga and Amman to join in this ritual. Non-participants offer support through donations, offerings and hospitality to processionists. This spirit of giving to others at times of celebration and of shared participation in rites believed to harness power and promote well being have helped, in the Mauritian context, to foster tolerance and to garner the store of ethnic cohabitation.

References

1. The research concerning kalimai in this article was carried out by Pavi Ramhota in 1993-4 and the material presented is based on anthropological field work in Mauritian villages.
2. The material concerning cavadee was based on interviews conducted jointly by Pavi Ramhota and Vishwanaden Govinden in 1997 and additional research concerning the historic role of cavadee in Mauritius was carried out by the latter.
3. MA RA 1276 Hindoos of Madras to Governor, 22 Nov 1854
4. Oral evidence, December 1997.

Conclusion

The stories which have been unfolded in this book have sought to underscore the interrelationships between groups which have served to facilitate the implantation of successive waves of immigrants into French and British Mauritius. Mauritian studies has been justly criticised for lacking an ideological approach. The present work has sought to demonstrate that through a more imaginative use of sources, the hidden histories of the constituent elements of *creoledom* can be illuminated and the ethnic myths of Mauritian origin effectively deconstructed.

Ethnic myths come in several forms. There are stereotypes rooted in old prejudices which have never been challenged, such as the notion of ethnically based aptitudes and hierarchies. The assumption that slaves of one 'caste' were more suitable for certain types of labour than another, or that slaves of different ethnic groups did not intermarry, have until now remained unquestioned. Other myths originate from the misinterpretation by historians of key documents or trends. Finally, ethnic mythologising arises from more recent community-based rivalries which seek to justify one group at the expense of another. Several such myths are called into question in this volume. Resistance to proselytism and cultural absorption are shown to have been functions of immigration-type and size of settling groups rather than of ethnic specificities, while minorities of both Asian and African origin have successively been integrated into larger communities.

The articles included in this volume pick up common themes in Mauritian social history. The French men who forged relationships with Coloured women in 18th century Isle of France, were responding to the same personal needs and economic advantages which 19th century Indian convicts and indentured immigrants, African liberated slaves and Chinese traders later perceived. These different groups encountered similar hostilities and penalties which did not however, succeed in frustrating their attempts to carve a niche in Mauritian colonial society. In so doing they gave rise to new communities of Coloureds, Creole-Chinese, Afro-Creoles and so on, who were themselves objects of prejudice and who integrated, in turn, into new social groupings. Throughout the successive struggles of immigrant populations to make their way in Mauritius, the contributions to this volume demonstrate that colonial policy diverged from practice at every turn, as the inhabitants of Mauritius defied their own laws or customs to enter mutually advantageous economic and social relationships with the new arrivals. The links forged between new immigrants and previous settlers created new forms of worship and modified mores, as Malabars and Chinese adapted to new religions without displacing a cultural heritage which continued to distinguish them from other social groups.

This work has also sought to emphasize the usually concealed side to the evolution of a colonial society generally typified by ethnic division and hierarchy and to delineate the overwhelming historical evidence of shared labour and shared lives. It was through such examples of co-operation and cohabitation that *creoledom* was forged in Mauritius. Whilst much of the material in this book has emphasised the gradual erasure of ethnic boundaries, it is also important to stress that *creoledom* as it has evolved in Mauritius should not imply the crass rejection of non-European models of identity but describes the process of elaboration of a distinctively Mauritian solution to the problem of creating a 'nation' with a 'national identity'. Mauritians have been quietly addressing this question for almost 300 years. Glimpses into the past lives of its inhabitants, such as this work has offered, have much to teach the analysts of the present.

Glossary

abir	*red powder*
adivasi	*tribal*
Ammen	*a female goddess worshipped by Hindus, especially Tamils*
annadanam	*the offering of food to devotees*
arrêté	*law, ordinance*
Arya Samaj	*Hindu reform movement*
Baharia Puja	*a rite worshipping goddess Kali, performed in an open space at a shrine*
balidan	*sacrifice(to deities), especially of animals*
bhajan	*devotional hymn (collectively sung)*
Brahma	*one of the Trinity of gods, less popular than Vishnu and Shiva*
carriole	*a horse-drawn carriage*
Cavadee	*A Tamil festival, and the name of the structures carried by devotees*
chowtal	*rigorous devotional songs*
Creole	*a person born in Mauritius, usually of mixed origin, except where used as a colonial term eg Creole Malabar, meaning a Malabar born in Mauritius*
creoledom	*the processes of adaptation of immigrants irrespective of ethnicity*
dacoity	*gang robbery*
dalit	*untouchable*
dan	*the act of giving*
dayn	*witch*
dhi	*a local guardian deity*

dhoti	*article of clothing worn by Indian men*
diya	*small earthen lamp*
Durga	*Hindu goddess and slayer of Mahishasura*
Guinée	*Designation for West Africans at the Isle of France*
grand dimoune	*Creole term of respect for Whites or important personages*
kodiyetum	*The raising of the flag on the first day of fasting for Tamil festivals*
lascar	*Sailor, generic term for Muslims in the Isle de France*
livre	*French currency prior to the Revolution*
Malabar	*Term used in the Isle of France to designate a person originating from the Indian subcontinent generally and Southern India in particular*
morcellement	*the parcelling out of lands to smallholders*
mulâtre	*A person of light skin colour; strictly defined as a 'half-caste'.*
izzat	*honour*
Kali	*Hindu goddess, worshipped in the kalimai shrine in Mauritius*
kansi	*goat*
kaptan	*term addressed to the White by the labourer*
kovil	*a South Indian Hindu temple*
longaniste	*sorceror, magician*
loupgarou	*werewolf*
mandir	*a Hindu temple*
ministre prince	*Creole term for the protector-deity*
Muruga	*a God worshipped by Saivist Tamils*
parab	*festival*
patrivatra	*devotion*
piastre	*Spanish silver coins used by traders in the Indian Ocean*

pioche	*hoe, term to use to designate slave field-hand*
prasad	*food ritually offered to a deity*
puja	*worship*
saheb	*a term used to address the White (planter)*
Saivism	*a branch of Hindu worship dedicated to Shiva*
Sanatanist	*orthodox Hindu*
sharam	*shame*
Shiva	*one of the two great gods of Hinduism*
sirdar	*labour supervisor, foreman*
supercargue	*an officer on board ship whose business is to manage the trade*
Tiroukkoural	*Hindu scriptures in the Tamil language*
Vaishnavism	*a form of Hindu worship dedicated to Vishnu*
Vishnu	*(alongside Shiva) one of the two great gods of Hinduism*

List of Abbreviations

ADR	Archives Départementales de la Réunion
ANOM	Archives Nationales d'Outre Mer
CO	Colonial Office
DFC	Dépôt des Fortifications des Colonies
EC	Etat Civil
PRO	Public Record Office
MA	Mauritius Archives
MGI	Mahatma Gandhi Institute

Bibliography

Allen, R. 1983 'Creoles, Indian Immigrants and the Restructuring of Society and Economy in Mauritius, 1767-1885' Illinois, PhD thesis

Allen, R. 1991 'Lives of neither Luxury nor Misery: Indians and Free Coloured Marginality on the Ile de France 1728-1810' *Rev. franc. d'hist. d'outre-mer*, t. LXXVIII, no 292

Allen, R. 1997 'Indian Immigrants and the Legacy of Marronage', *Itinerario*, vol 21, no 1

Bassier, W.M.Z. 1987 'Kali-Mai Worship in Guyana: A Quest for a New Identity', in *Indians in the Caribbean*, I.J. Bahadur Singh (ed.) London: Oriental University Press

Bernardin de Saint Pierre, J.B. 1983 *Voyage à l' Isle de France*, Editions La Decouverte, Paris

Callikhan-Proag, A. 1984 'La representation des Immigrants Indiens dans le Cernéen, 1836-72', in Bissoondoyal & Servansingh (eds) *Indians Overseas: the Mauritian Experience*, MGI

Carter, M. 1990 'An elite in servility?: Indian slaves in Mauritius, 1729-1834', *Indian Historical Review*, Vol XV. Special Issue: The World of Slavery

Carter, M. 1994 *Lakshmi's Legacy: Testimonies of Indian Women in 19th Century Mauritius*, EOI, Stanley

Carter, M. 1995 *Servants, Sirdars & Settlers: Indians in Mauritius, 1834-1874*, New Delhi, Oxford University Press

Carter, M. 1996 *Voices from Indenture; Experiences of Indian Migrants in the British Empire*, London, Leicester University Press

Carter, M. & Ng Foong Kwong, J. 1997 *Forging the Rainbow: Labour Immigrants in British Mauritius*, Terre Rouge

Deerr, N. 1942 *The History of Sugar*, Vol 1, Chapman and Hall Ltd. London

De Rauville, H. 1908 *L'Isle de France Contemporaine,* La Nouvelle Librairie Nationale, Paris

Dictionnaire de Biographie Mauricienne, 1947-1997, Société d' Histoire de L' Ile Maurice, Mauritius, various years d'Unienville, Baron *Statistique de l'Ile Maurice et ses Dependances*, 3 vols, Mauritius, 1885

d'Unienville, R. 1975 *Histoire Politique de l'Isle de France, Vol. 1*, Port Louis

d'Unienville, R. 1979a *Hier Suffren*, Port Louis

d'Unienville, R. 1979b 'Le Statut Juridique des Immigrants à l'Ile Maurice' in *Mouvements de Populations dans l'Océan Indien*, Paris Libraire Honoré Champion.

d'Unienville, R. 1982 *Histoire Politique de l'Isle de France, Vol 2*, Port Louis

Dupon, J. F. 1977 *Contraintes Insulaires et Fait Colonial aux Mascareignes et aux Seychelles*, III vols., Paris

Emrith, M. 1994 *A History of the Muslims in Mauritius*, ELP Ltée, Vacoas

Filliot, J-M. 1974 *La traite des esclaves vers les Mascareignes au XVIIIe siècle*, Paris

Gerbeau, H. 1989 'The Indians of the Mascarenes, A Success in Diaspora: Mauritius and Reunion (17th-20th centuries)', unpublished conference paper, Delhi

Jahangeer-Chojoo, A. 1997 'La Communauté Musulmane à Port Louis. Une Etude de Géographie Sociale', thèse de 3ème cycle, Bordeaux

Jumeer, M. 1984 'Les Affranchis et les Indiens libres à l'Ile de France au XVIIIe siècle (1721 - 1803)', thèse de doctorat de 3e cycle, Poitiers

Khan, A. 1977 'Kali-mai Puja in Guyana', *Religion*, 7: 35-45

Lal, B.V. 1984 'Labouring Men and Nothing More: Some Problems of Indian Indenture in Fiji', in Kay Saunders (ed.), *Indentured Labour in the British Empire, 1834-1920*, London, Croom Helm

Lubbock, B. 1955 *Coolie Ships and Oil Sailers*, Glasgow

Ly Tio Fane, H. 1983 *La Diaspora Chinoise dans l'océan Indien Occidental*, EOI, Mauritius

Ly Tio Fane, H. 1995 unpublished paper, conference on 'The Concept of Mauritian Studies', MGI, Mauritius

Mandelbaum, D.G. 1988 *Women's Seclusion and Men's Honor; Sex Roles in North India, Bangladesh, and Pakistan*, Tucson, University of Arizona Press

Maxwell-Stewart, H. 1997 'Convict Workers, 'Penal Labour' and Sarah Island:

Life at Macquarie Harbour, 1822-1834', in Ian Duffield & James Bradley (eds), *Representing Convicts; New Perspectives on Convict Forced Labour Migration,* London, Leicester University Press

Myer, N. 1990 *Reconstructing the Black Past; Blacks in Britain 1780-1830*, London, Frank Cass

Macmillan, A. 1910 *Mauritius Illustrated*, London

Moutou, B. 1996 *Les Chrétiens de L'Ile Maurice*, Port Louis

Milbert, M. J. 1812 *Voyage Pittoresque à l'Ile de France, au Cap du Bonne Espérance et à l'Ile de Teneriffe*, Paris

Nagapen, A. 1984 *The Indian Christian Community in Mauritius*, Port Louis

Nagapen, A. 1987 'Les Indiens à l'Ile de France: Acculturation ou Deculturation?' in *Historical and Cultural Relations between France and India, XVIIth-XXth Centuries*, 2 vols, Réunion

Nagapen, A. 1991 *A l'Aube de la Mission Catholique Chinoise à l'île Maurice 1873-1945*, Port Louis

Nagapen, A. 1996 *Histoire de l'Eglise Isle de France - Ile Maurice, 1721-1968*, Port Louis

Nagapen, A. 1996 *Histoire de la Colonie Isle de France - Ile Maurice 1721-1968*, Port Louis

Napal, D. 1965. *Les Indiens à l'Ile de France*, Ile Maurice

Ng Foong Kwong, J. 1989 'Les Hakkas a l'Ile Maurice', Mémoire de maitrise, Université de la Réunion

Ng Foong Kwong, J. 1996 ' La Naissance du Commerce Chinois, 1826-1875', DEA, Réunion

Nicholas, S. & Shergold, R. 1988 'Transportation as Global Migration', in Stephen Nicholas (ed.), *Convict Workers; Reinterpreting Australia's Past,* Cambridge, Cambridge University Press

Noel, K. 1991 *L'Esclavage à l'Isle de France*, Editions Two Cities, Paris

North Coombes, M.D. 1990 'Indentured Labour in the Sugar Industries of Natal and Mauritius, 1834-1910', in Bhana, S. (ed) *Essays on Indentured Indians in Natal*, Durban

Phillips, L. 1960. 'Kali-Mai puja', *Timehri,* xxxix: 37-46

Sooriamoorthy, R. 1977 *Les Tamouls à L'Ile Maurice*, Port Louis

Teelock, V. 1995 *Slaves Speak Out: The Testimony of Slaves in the Era of Sugar*, African Cultural Centre, Bell Village

Tinker, H. 1974 *A New System of Slavery*, Oxford University Press

Toussaint, A. 1972 *Histoire des Iles Mascareignes*, Paris

Toussaint, A. 1979 'Le Role des Femmes dans les Migrations', *Mouvements de Populations dans l'Océan Indien*, Paris, Honore Champion

Vertovec, S. 1992 *Hindu Trinidad: Religion, Ethnicity and Socio-Economic Change*, London, Macmillan

Notes on Contributors

Clare Anderson has recently completed a doctoral thesis on the immigration of Indian convicts. She is a lecturer at the University of Leicester, UK.

Marina Carter holds a doctorate in history from the University of Oxford. She is a freelance historian.

Raymond d'Unienville has written extensively on the political history of the Isle of France. He is a barrister.

Vishwanaden Govinden is a specialist on Indian immigration in Mauritius. He is employed at the Immigration Archive of the Mahatma Gandhi Institute.

James Ng Foong Kwong holds a DEA from the University of Reunion. He is a lecturer at the Mahatma Gandhi Institute, researching on Chinese immigration to Mauritius.

Pavi Ramhota has an MSc in anthropology from the London School of Economics. He is a lecturer at the Mahatma Gandhi Institute.